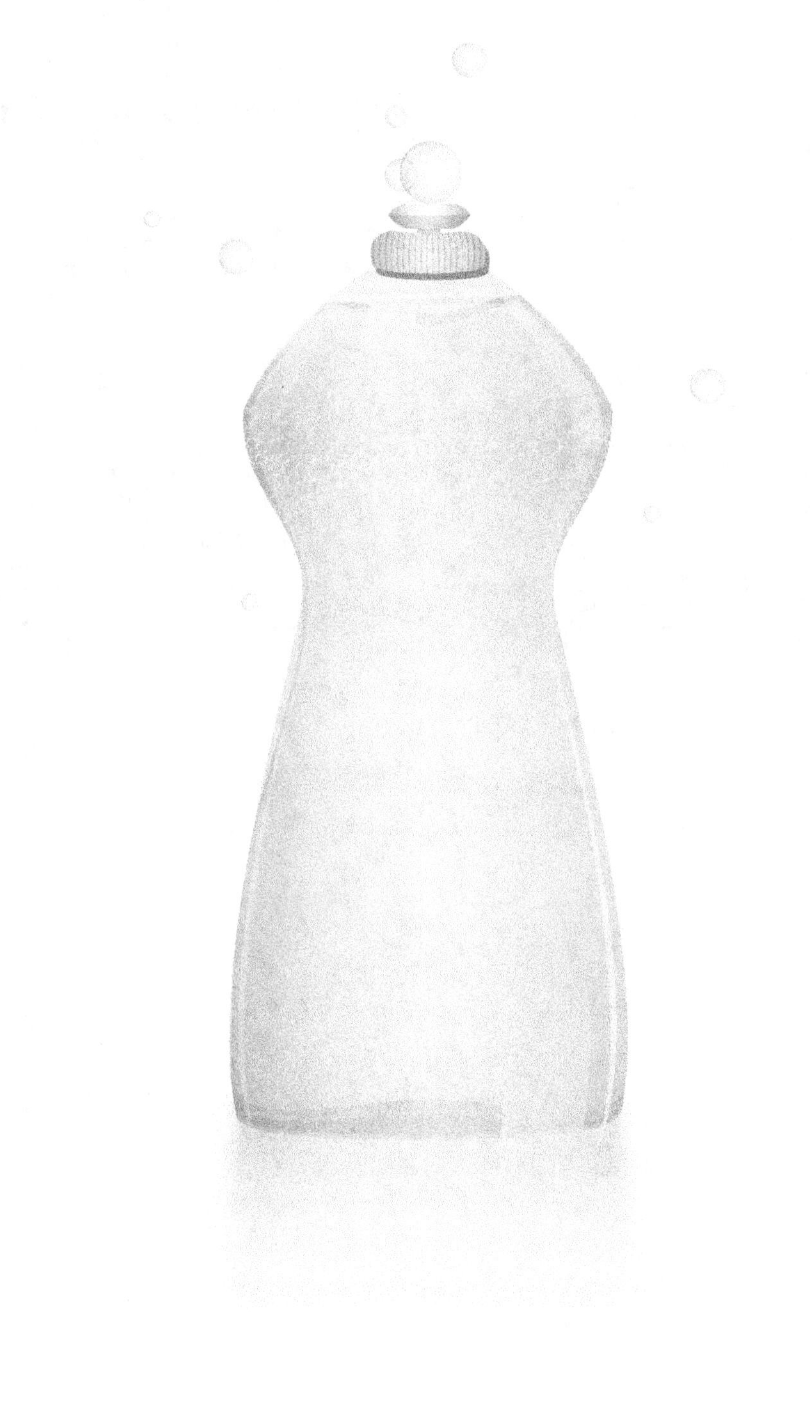

Confessions of a Skittish Catholic from Idaho

Naked Joy

To protect the privacy of certain individuals the names and identifying details have been changed.

Cover and Interior design by www.wisdomhousebooks.com

Manufactured in the United States of America

For more information:

www.NakedJoyBook.com

Paperback ISBN: 978-0-9977795-1-6

Hardback ISBN: 978-0-9977795-0-9

EBook ISBN: 978-0-9977795-2-3

LCCN: 2016918528

BIOGRAPHY & AUTOBIOGRAPHY / Personal Essay / Creative Non Fiction

Table of Contents

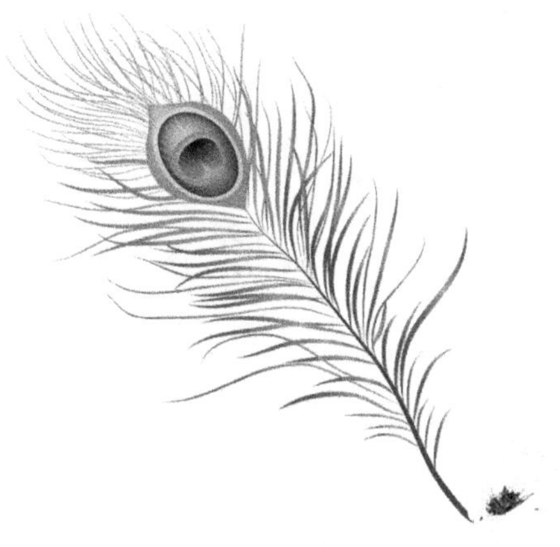

This book is dedicated to Preston Baker.

It is mostly his fault.

I'd also like to give myself some credit—
for refusing to give up.

Prologue

The psychiatrist's name is Doctor Wise and I hope he is. Posing as a stable person, I phone his office located in a nearby hospital, and shudder when a raspy female voice barks at me. "Ma'am, whatever you do, once inside our building, you'd better enter the double doors to the right of the reception desk. Take the opposite doors and you'll be committed to the psychiatric ward, no questions asked."

I mask my flaring anxiety with a light-hearted chuckle, as if I were a cool, breezy woman hardly in need of psychiatric care much less being locked up. After my appointment is confirmed for the following Tuesday, I hang up and scurry to the toilet.

"The *right* doors are *right*," I repeat to myself, and it crosses my mind that the doctor, after our initial visit, might personally escort me through those opposite, one-way doors to lunacy.

The morning of my appointment I arrive at the hospital early and enter the doors to the RIGHT, my eyes scanning the foyer in search of robotic people in white coats zooming towards me, in case I have panicked and confused my directions. But there's no one in sight; I take a seat outside the office marked "Thomas N. Wise, MD."

Fumbling through an old *Psychology Today* magazine, my right heel bounces uncontrollably as I madly pick at a hangnail, glance at my watch, and remind myself to breathe.

Once the door opens a tall, grandfatherly man with wispy white hair and a skim-milk complexion welcomes me into his office. He extends his hand as he looks directly into my eyes, in search of madness, I am guessing, since that's his job. We talk amidst piles of papers, stacks of books, half-empty Styrofoam cups, dusty photos of people I don't know but assume are important. The air is musty. I worry that this cluttered room is an indication of the doctor's state of mind, but assure myself he is such a prominent, busy man he has no interest in tidiness.

Our conversation consumes most of an hour and the shrink shows emotion, audibly gasping, only when I share the cause of my first full-blown anxiety attack, twenty years earlier while living in Tokyo.

"My daughter was just three months old when our German au pair intentionally broke both her tiny arms." The man's mouth falls open and he grabs the Kleenex box, pulling one for each of us. I blubber the story as best I can as the grief I've been repressing for years overwhelms me like the worst of nightmares.

The shaken man says something I vaguely hear about my understandable state of angst and how much I must have suffered. He squirms in his chair and seems so uncomfortable I am compelled to comfort him as I dry my eyes.

"On a lighter note, what a great name you have as a doctor," I tease.

Feigning a grin, he quips "Nah, I thought the same thing in my youth, but soon learned it comes from German and means 'pale and pasty.'"

"Well, the name fits," I am tempted to add, my mood brightening. But instead I lead him back to our talk about my anxious state and what might be done about it.

I am hardly surprised by his diagnosis; I don't need a professional to tell me people like myself, cursed with Generalized Anxiety Disorder, or G.A.D, plow through life with exaggerated worries and tension, often when there is no real reason.

To the best of my knowledge, I have never been shot, stabbed, caught in a burning building, kidnapped, raped, or hit by a truck, yet I habitually worry about such catastrophes. In fact, I grow anxious if I am not worried, believing something must be very wrong, or will be at any moment.

"Well, G.A.D. is not uncommon in an individual like yourself, Miss Kilmer," the shrink reassures me. "Especially given the horrible event you've just described to me. Add post traumatic stress to your inherent propensity to worry, and I am surprised you are functioning." I fake a chuckle and he smiles like he truly cares.

"I perceive you to be intense, bright, and creative, which is not uncommon for an individual with significant anxiety issues. The disorder is twice as likely to occur in women as men. Admittedly, it can be quite debilitating, though you seem resilient, and we do have very effective forms of treatment these days."

I question to myself whether the doctor is simply being tactful with his flattering description, so as to avoid telling me I am stark, raving mad. And I ponder expensive little pills and unpleasant side effects like blurred vision, twitching, memory loss, excessive thirst and frequent urination.

"Anything else you'd like to talk about today?" he asks. "And may I call you Nan?"

I realize my hour is almost over and Dr. Wise seems convinced I do not belong behind those ominous doors to the left.

"You can call me anything you'd like. And I guess I should tell you that for years I have lived with my anxiety, trying not to allow a shaky temperament to interrupt my day-to-day life. But recently a sparrow held me hostage in a Bermuda hotel bathroom for over an hour, almost forcing me to miss an important business dinner. I'd left the sliding doors open to invite the ocean breeze, and he swooped in as well. I had no choice but to lock myself in the bathroom. Why lock the door? Well, I wasn't thinking rationally and I could have lost my job. I suppose that's why I decided to come here today."

Dr. Wise looks up from his lap and furrows his brow. "Are we talking about a phobic reaction here, Nan?"

"You're asking me?" I wonder.

I am prompted to take him back to my sophomore year in college and a behavioral psychology class required for my major. Dr. Heinz Klatt, our professor, informed us on the first day that we would be undertaking operational conditioning on the behavior of pigeons, and upon presenting a bird to the class, I fainted. He thus instructed me to stay afterwards to discuss my reaction to birds and how I might complete the course. The professor's efforts at desensitizing me to the creature were in vain, and in the end my lab partner did all the handling of our subject that semester, a flighty pigeon we called "Robin."

Having listened intently, the doctor shares some wisdom. "A phobia, from the Greek word meaning fear, is learned from an actual experience. When a person is in a highly emotional state, the ability to learn is accelerated, and the mind quickly figures out what is needed to avoid what seems like danger. Often, a phobia occurs after exposure to what is perceived as a frightening object or situation, but sometimes the cause is simply obsessive thinking about such fears.

"There are hundreds if not thousands of identified phobias, from fear of clocks to fear of peanut butter sticking to the top of one's mouth, to fear of knees. Other more common yet still illogical fears are of spiders, open spaces, vomit, germs, bridges, refrigerators, water, and even fear itself.

"Your rather extreme reaction to our fine feathered friends, Nan, leads me to believe you are, to use the scientific term, *ornithophobic*. I suggest you see a colleague of mine, a woman specializing in anxiety disorders, including phobias. I believe she can help you get a handle on your problem. After you have seen her three times, phone and tell me how you are faring. Best of luck, and I look forward to hearing from you."

At which point Dr. Wise scavenges through the overflowing top drawer of his desk. Within moments, he hands me a dog-eared business card, with the name and number of the psychologist he is recommending to me.

I drive home feeling more relaxed than I've been in months, comforted by the fact that my neurotic condition is documented in chapters of psychology books and that I am not technically crazy.

Over the next few weeks I give serious consideration to the doctor's suggestions, pros and cons. In the end, I increase the intensity of my gym workouts, take up yoga, attempt meditation, drink more wine, and resume writing my stories.

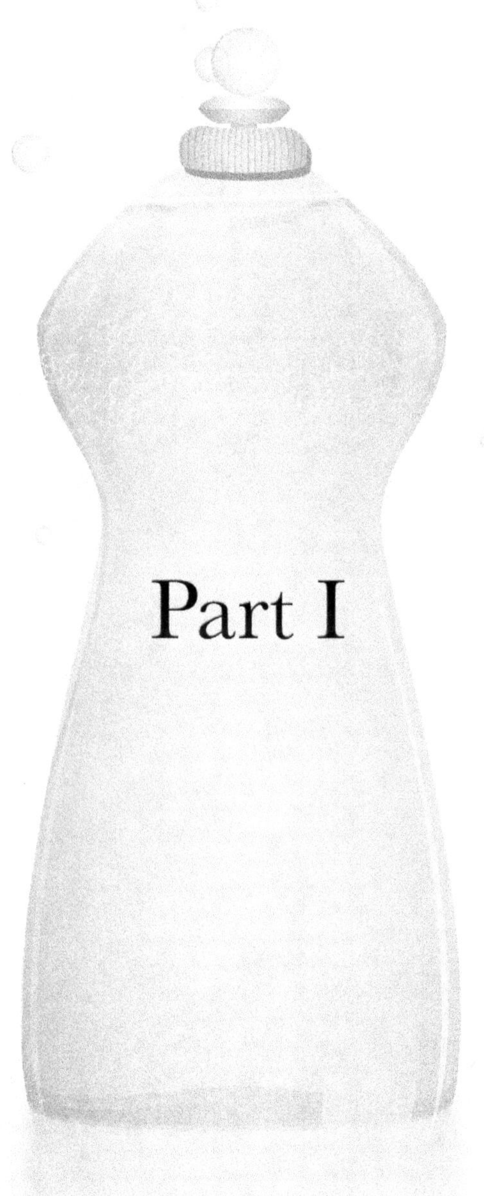

Part I

Idaho Roots

The peacock is massive, and I am four. He's there now, behind the haystack; I sense him. Instinctively, I turn and bolt across the barnyard towards the house. The screaming fowl lunges after me, exploding into a kaleidoscope of feathers, a giant fan of terror. Stumbling through a jungle of loose gravel and panic, I look to Mommy watching from Aunt Millie's porch, and realize she is doubled over with laughter.

Aunt Millie's farmhouse pops into view on the left as we crest a hill on Fargo Road, a ribbon of a country lane unraveling west out of Nampa, Idaho, toward the Oregon border.

Nampa was planted amidst the sagebrush in the late 1800s, when towns were popping up every few miles along the Oregon Short Line, connecting Wyoming to Oregon. The smudge on the map that would become my hometown was as good a spot as any for weary travelers to recuperate for the night.

Some say Nampa was named after an Indian chief whose name

meant Big Foot, because his tribe stuffed their moccasins with sagebrush to keep their feet warm, making their footprints larger than normal. Others claim Nampa is the Indian word for moccasin, while still others admit they don't have a clue where the name originated, but there is also a Nampa in Canada, so maybe it was borrowed.

Maybe it does not mean anything at all.

With the ambiguous motto "What a Place to Live," Nampa lies less than twenty miles southwest of Boise, the state capital and "City of Trees." Driving in from the north, just after the small, black and white sign flashes past to the right reading "Entering Nampa, Population 19,311" I envision the huge, red, black, yellow and white billboard as if it still loomed on the left, with ten bowling pins rocketing in all directions. In the boldest of letters, the sign greeted motorists:

"WELCOME TO NAMPA, HOME OF NAMPA BOWL!"

I've never really taken to bowling, the narrow lanes crowding on top of each other, smoke-hazed air, roaring balls, and crashing pins. I feel a headache coming on just thinking about this pastime enjoyed by many Americans.

I never really took to Nampa either. It wasn't a pretty place at all. In fact, it was dry, flat, and rather dismal, punctuated by an inescapable odor billowing from the nearby "Amalgamated Sugar Beet Factory," where huge vats of stubborn beets are smooshed, ground, and simmered into pure, refined "White Satin Sugar"—Nampa's finest.

It's the kind of pungent aroma that makes visitors to the area blurt, "Oh my God! What is that smell?"

The beet processing goes on for months, but eventually, when the factory gears wind down for the year and the beets are pulverized, most Nampans are so accustomed to the stench they seem to hardly notice it's gone.

Like it or not, Nampa was home. My father was born and raised there until, as a scrawny teenager, he headed off to fight in the Second World War. He met my mother in her hometown of Atlantic City, after he had returned stateside and was unwinding at the beach. They soon married and a year later my older brother Biff was born. Before my mother had time to reconsider, they packed up a 1947 black Plymouth sedan and drove across the country to Nampa, where Mom cried for nearly a year before accepting her version of hell as home.

Not that her childhood in New Jersey had been idyllic. Abandoned by her father when she was small, the young girl was raised by her feisty little Irish grandmother, while her mother worked outside the home at some job I don't recall. From her endless stories, it sounds like my mother grew up making the most of life, enjoying all her hometown had to offer, like the beach, the famous Steel Pier with its high diving horse and annual Miss America pageant, and summers full of friendly tourists and sometimes famous celebrities. She carved a good time out of a less-than-ideal situation, haunted by thoughts of a father she never knew.

Once transplanted to the "wild west," the eastern sophisticate eventually grew accustomed to small town life far away from her friends and family, and added three more children to her nest. She rightly accused Nampa of being primitive, "Podunk" she liked to call it, but it did not stop her from striving to raise an ideal family, the kind she never had. She taught us east coast ways like white gloves for church, pearls for Sunday dinners, and ballroom dancing, all novelties in Idaho at the time. The petite, strong-willed, strict disciplinarian focused on creating a picture perfect life for us, and I felt pressured to measure up.

While Atlantic City proudly hosted the annual Miss America Pageant, Nampa was home every summer to the Snake River Stampede—"The Wildest, Fastest Show on Earth!" In 1937, the popular bucking bull contest broke away from the annual Harvest Festival, and its "rootin' tootin'" participants joined the Professional Rodeo Cowboys Association. Then, in 1950, a gigantic, horseshoe-shaped, grass-green wooden stadium was constructed just north of town, with a seating capacity of 10,000—half the town of Nampa!

It isn't often I am tempted to brag about my hometown, but over the years, top notch cow pokes from around the country have come to Nampa each July to participate in the Stampede, which today has grown to be one of the top ten rodeos on the circuit.

Early on, glitzy Hollywood cowboy singers like Gene Autry, Roy Rogers, and Rex Allen were brought into town to perform at the rodeo, in an attempt to fill the arena with spectators each night. Later, when that genre of hunky, wild west movie stars was dwindling, dreamy television actors like *Bonanza's* "Little Joe" Cartwright, *Gunsmoke's* Marshall Dillon, and my favorite, the mysterious, masked Lone Ranger and his Apache sidekick, Tonto, were hired to lure fans to Nampa's event of the year.

By the eighties, few pretty cowboys capable of carrying a tune were to be found, so the Stampede turned to Country Western singers as the entertainment draw. The last I was in town at rodeo time must've been the mid-eighties, when a handsome, if not rugged Glen Campbell crooned his country western tunes every night that week in July, from the sappy "Gentle on my Mind" to the peppier "Rhinestone Cowboy" hits. It struck me that for many of the hometown citizens, such glamour and excitement must have been as intoxicating as a night out at the **Derail**, a popular watering hole not far from the railroad station.

Every evening before the rodeo started, a seemingly endless pageant of flamboyantly dressed cowboys, girls and bubble-nosed clowns paraded through downtown Nampa. The horses carpeted our streets with pungent, fresh manure, en route to the Stampede grounds.

My Grandpa Kilmer counted aloud the number of horses clomping past us, which was usually several hundred. As he counted I watched in disgust as the skittish horses arched their long hairy tails, dumping what seemed like a ton of poop on our town, adding to its distinctive aroma. The only night my parents did not insist we drive downtown to witness the free parade was the evening we attended the rodeo, where we could catch the grand finale inside the arena, decked out in our hand-me-down cowboy hats, vests, chaps and boots.

One year the late heartthrob Michael Landon, who played the youngest brother Little Joe Cartwright on the hit TV series *Bonanza*, starred at the Stampede. I was working at the time as a lifeguard at the local golf course, loosely referred to as the country club, when the celebrity unexpectedly dropped by for a swim. Every female over the age of five was deliriously giddy watching this hunk rub baby oil over his muscular torso, while hardly noticing the Barbie doll of a wife at his side. With each perfect dive he sliced into the sparkling water, the Adonis set hearts pounding.

Little Joe's historic swim was without doubt the highlight of rodeo week that summer, at least for those of us lucky enough to have been at the pool that dream-like afternoon. Other than the stampede, Nampa offered little excitement the other fifty-one weeks of the year, at least on the surface . . .

The iconic Sugar Beet Factory stinking up the Treasure Valley.

The author, age 4, visiting Aunt Millie's sheep. Wilder, Idaho.

Home Bodies

If one didn't suspect dead babies might be buried behind the bed, our home seemed like a perfectly nice place to live.

The grey, wood-shingled, four bedroom house on the corner was pleasant and comfortable by most standards, but impressive compared to many of the smaller, less-spacious homes in the neighborhood. My parents had bought the place from Doc Ross, our family physician who delivered three of the four Kilmer siblings. His own children were grown so he and his elegant wife Margaret decided to downsize.

My bedroom was a haven and most of my time indoors was spent there. Two tall windows looked out at a majestic cherry tree, its lofty branches supporting a wooden tree house my older brother Biff had built. I was not allowed up into his sacred shack, but sometimes I spied as he and his buddies sat up in the tree munching cherries then tossing pits onto the ground below. I couldn't really hear all of their conversation, just a lot of guffawing from those crazy boys.

Sometimes I saw smoke coming from their hideout, but I never snitched—not on my idolized older brother.

At first, my room was pink and frilly with white wooden furniture and dolls perched across the pillows. Later, in high school, I chose a black and white theme for a more grown-up look. The walls were papered in checks, the windows curtained in polka dots and the shades, striped. It is a wonder I could think in that room much less sleep.

One constant was a white wicker vanity propped against the wall opposite the windows. A large mirror hung over the table and the stool twirled in circles if I felt inclined. There I did most of my writing—poetry, diary entries, letters, school papers. Occasionally I'd glance up at myself in the mirror. I liked the way I looked while hard at work, even if things did, at times, appear backwards.

A hidden feature of my room was a tiny closet, about three feet high by two feet wide, tucked into the wall behind my bed. My father told me this was a pipe closet which led to the tub in the bathroom next door, built so the plumbing could be repaired without having to tear up the wall. Because it was kept locked, I couldn't be sure what lurked below as I tried to sleep at night. But I sometimes used the closet and my warped imagination to manipulate my bratty younger brother. Luring him under the bed to get a look at the secret compartment, I'd threaten the kid. "Do you remember what I told you is behind that wall?" Shaking his head knowingly, I'd reiterate. "This is where we put the chopped-up bodies of little boys we had before you. Little boys who misbehaved and did not do what their big sister told them to do!"

This may sound cruel, but it worked nearly every time I needed to get my rascal of a brother in line, at least until he was old enough to be able to pry open the closet door to find nothing but old, rusty pipes. By then he was out of my control, but at least I slept better at night, knowing what was really behind that mysterious little door.

Our house was within walking distance of our parochial school, St. Paul's; our dentist, the buck-toothed Dr. Norton who yanked out too many of my permanent teeth; and odd orthodontist Dr. Gold whose office was adjacent to his dark, eerie, mock-castle style house. I dreaded those times when, after jerking, twisting and snipping the tiny wires around my soon to be aching teeth, he lured me into his creepy house.

"Let's take a peek inside and give a snappy hello to June bug!" I can almost hear him threatening. He wanted to show his wife June my eyes, which he apparently found haunting. Judging from their home, they enjoyed being haunted.

"Follow me, dear," Mrs. Gold would whisper in her raspy voice as she led me down the narrow, blurry hallway to their dimly-lit den. Bookshelves lined the stuffy room, and from the top shelves a collection of pasty, slant-eyed Japanese dolls displayed in glass boxes stared down at me. The figures were garishly dressed and on their heads sat fake-looking, waxy black wiglets.

"Doc and I bought these on one of our deluxe trips to the Orient, sweet pea. Aren't they just yummy?"

Then the creepy woman would pluck a tissue from between her mushy breasts and tenderly dab her murky eyes.

June used the word "yummy" to describe everything from her dolls to my eyes to the Pacific blue Cadillac in their driveway, which my dad claimed he actually paid for, given the amount of money he spent for my years of orthodontic treatment.

Held captive inside their version of home, I feigned a smile and did my best not to look horrified at the ghastly, glass-caged dolls, or at scary, swollen Mrs. Gold. Her bleached yellow hair reminded me of the scratchy bails of straw in my Aunt Millie's barnyard, and her beady little grey eyes oozed a yellowish fluid thicker than tears as she led me around her house, which I imagined to be haunted.

"June Bug" often wore a Muumuu, a brightly-colored, loose fitting frock she'd picked up on their latest vacation to the Hawaiian Islands. As she swished around the house, a floating head above her tent-like gown, I wondered what might be going on under all that billowing fabric, and this was not all I wondered about my orthodontist's scary wife.

Unnerved by yet another monthly visit to check my wired mouth, I usually walked home, roughly twelve blocks through a typical middle class neighborhood of modest homes and well-tended yards. Nampa was a safe little town, so few parents thought twice about allowing their kids to roam the streets unsupervised.

It was springtime and I was about nine years old, when a crazed looking old guy about twenty appeared from behind some shrubs and began heckling me.

"I'm gonna get you, little girl!" he hollered.

I took off running, not knowing if he was serious or just high on Coors beer or drugs. I sped home as fast as my short legs would carry me, losing one of my church shoes along the way.

My mother was not happy when it came time for mass the following Sunday morning and I came out of my room wearing only one black, patent-leather "Mary Jane."

I ended up embarrassed at mass that day, trying to hide my feet in ballet-slippers.

We kids could walk to the Carnegie Library, downtown shops like the Idaho Department Store, Penny-Wise Drugs, Nampa Floral, and Schmitt's Shoe Shop. Schmitt's is where, as one of my chores, I was assigned to pick up freshly polished shoes, re-woven purses and belts with an added hole whenever Dad had put on a few pounds. I never minded the job as Mr. Schmitt was a nice man who always had a joke and a piece of hard candy for me, and I loved the sign over his cluttered counter: "Early to bed, early to rise, work like hell, and advertise."

Maybe Mr. Schmitt's inspiring sign is the reason I ended up working in advertising later in life.

A movie theater called The Pix was within walking distance of our house. Right next door was another theater, The Majestic, which mysteriously caught fire in the sixties so was boarded up and empty for years. My siblings and I always suspected The Pix owner might have been involved in The Majestic's demise, but we were never able to come up with any solid evidence so eventually gave up on the notion.

On Saturday afternoons during the school year we Kilmer kids liked to walk downtown to the "Pix" for a picture show. I was not allowed to accompany my older brother and sister to the movies until I was in first grade, and I looked forward to this day for what seemed like forever in my preschooler's mind.

We usually paid for our tickets with a milk bottle lid and maybe a dime, which must have been a promotional deal for the local dairy, run by the father of a classmate, Jerald Shiller, who claimed milk and cheese made him sick. Today he'd probably be considered lactose intolerant.

One of the first movies I saw at The Pix was a sixties farce called *Cinderfella* starring the zany Jerry Lewis of the Muscular Dystrophy Telethon fame. It was not so much the slapstick humor or spoof on the original fairytale that captivated me, but the glamour of Beverly Hills, where the movie supposedly took place.

Although Jerry is a clumsy simpleton in the movie, he lives in a large, luxuriously furnished mansion. Each morning, he simply reaches out the kitchen window and plucks oranges from the tree for his wicked step family's breakfast. The poor guy has to sneak into the sparkling swimming pool on the lush grounds, which he is forced to clean each day. There, floating on an air mattress one dreamy afternoon, he meets his fairy godfather played by the late, lovable Ed Wynn, and magic ensues.

Cinderfella seemed to find comfort within the realm of fantasy, and I could relate.

Wasted

As incredible as it might seem, a palace stood amidst the sagebrush, sugar beets, and stench of our town. I like to imagine bleary-eyed travelers arriving in Nampa in the early 1900s, believing they were seeing a mirage at the sight of this majestic structure.

The Dewey Palace Hotel graced downtown Nampa from 1902 until its demise in 1963. According to my Grandpa Kilmer, who migrated with his young wife Hazel to Idaho from Minnesota in the 1920s, a flamboyant, wheeler-dealer by the name of Colonel W.C. Dewey, got reckless and ended up in Nampa around the turn of the century. This controversial character, nicknamed "Con," had been charged with murdering a guy in a shoot-out in Silver City, a tiny mining town in central Idaho. As a result he spent time in the state pen. Grandpa said that "Con" not only managed to get out of prison, but to make a fortune mining silver and gold in Idaho.

Perhaps because no one else would have him, the calculating colonel decided to build his dream place in downtown Nampa. His palace was his home and an accommodating oasis for weary, cross-country rail travelers. The colonel was not able to enjoy his new home for long, as he died suddenly from unknown causes in 1903, leaving his last million dollars to his only son.

People say that at the time, in the early 1900s, the Dewey Palace was the grandest, most luxurious hotel in all the country between Omaha, Nebraska, and Portland, Oregon. This notion captivated me and my neighbor, a skinny kid about my age named Willie. Every few months or so, he and I would get the urge to check on the colonel's palatial home. I'd fib to my parents, "Me and Willie are riding our bikes to the library to get some books—is it okay if we aren't back before dark?"

"Don't worry, take your time. If anyone grabs you, they will drop you at the first lamp post," my mother would chide. I sometimes wondered if she was kidding or not.

By that time most of the property had been condemned, and we knew we were trespassing by sneaking around the grounds. Unable to resist the temptation, we'd park our bikes in the rusty racks outside the library, so if our parents drove by they'd be convinced we were inside. Gingerly crossing the street like a couple of prowlers, we'd slip around to the back of the hotel where no one could spot us. From there we could gaze up at the magnificent building and fantasize about its grand interior—once the stage of spectacular events cast with fascinating figures from the past. Right there in Nampa!

Old Pictures of The Dewey Palace confirm the red brick mansion was three stories tall; each tier embraced by a generous, wrap-around veranda resting on stately, carved columns. Two identical towers crowned with bell-shaped domes sheathed in shiny copper, rose above the roofline at either end of the building, which took up an entire city block. On certain evenings at dusk, in just the right lighting, it appeared to my young imagination that the domes were two giant bells suspended from the heavens. I could almost hear their glorious chimes ringing throughout our drowsy little town.

Once in a while Willie and I mustered up the courage to creep up close to the foundation and peek through the cracks in the warped, old boards covering the basement windows. We could make out what appeared to be the cluttered remains of what had to have been a bowling alley, probably Nampa's first.

We identified a spacious billiard room, some sort of beauty parlor, grimy, old-fashioned restrooms with pull-chain flushers and a lot of blank, open space. The upper stories of the mansion had to be furnished by our young imaginations, making splendor and opulence free from the limitations reality imposed.

Sorry to say, the Dewey Palace did not survive Nampa. Progressive, civic-minded citizens destroyed it. The "Razing of the Dewey Palace" was how town officials referred to this sacrilege. And today there is surprisingly little mention of this extraordinary palace in Idaho history books.

There seemed to be no reasonable, sane explanation for destroying one of Nampa's few shots at historical significance. I do recall vague stirrings of protest about renovating rather than destroying this magnificent piece of architecture, but to no avail. A demolition team leveled the massive building and in a matter of days, amidst a crowd of curious citizens including me and Willie, who watched through teary eyes. Within months it seemed, the First Security Bank ascended from the site. And within a matter of years, few gave much thought at all to the spectacular Dewey Palace Hotel—Nampa's brief exposure to grandeur.

It wasn't so much the new bank's efficient drive-through windows or the nifty automatic glass doors or the garish artwork depicting local scenic vistas that excited most Nampans. Rather, it was the first asphalt-covered, spacious, free parking lot adjacent to the bank that had people talking. Prior to that time Nampa offered only metered parking at the curb of the street. I remember that the gray, steel meters lined up like soldiers outside the post office, public library, and downtown stores offered either fifteen or thirty minute parking, usually at an angle as opposed to parallel. Mom would toss me a fat silver nickel for fifteen minutes, or a slender dime for half an hour in the space.

"Hop to it, Nanner!" she'd command.

"Fifteen minutes should do it if we get moving! And a penny saved is a penny earned."

Obligingly, I would slide the coin into the slot on the meter, twist the metal dial half a circle, and watch with satisfaction as the little red metal flag warning "VIOLATION!" disappeared from the small window in the meter.

Those time frames on the parking meters were a good indicator of the types of business transactions that took place in downtown Nampa back then. Nothing more complicated than a fifteen to thirty minute transaction took place in the sleepy town I called home.

As my life progressed through junior high and high school, the town forged on. The authorities continued to demolish old, relatively charming buildings only to asphalt the vacant lots and convert them into coveted, off-street parking.

Consequently, downtown merchants were driven out of town so headed west towards Mecca, officially known as Karcher Mall, the exciting new shopping center under construction on Nampa-Caldwell Boulevard, not far from the aromatic sugar beet factory.

By 1965, "Mall" was a new word in Nampan's vocabulary. At last we could shop in air-conditioned comfort, and park for free.

"Meet me at the mall!" was all the rage. For several decades it was *the* place to gather, until Boise Town Square was built, drawing business away from Karcher Mall and into the state capital nearly twenty miles away. Poor Karcher Mall still struggles today to stay afloat.

A major overhaul of our town's sewage treatment plant was another major civic project in the late seventies. This essential facility, its fumes competing with those of the sugar beet factory, was updated at that time. Upon its completion several years later, Nampa could boast of the largest, most modern, odorless waste management facility in Idaho, nicknamed the "Gem State" apparently for reasons other than its waste management.

I must've cringed upon reading in the *Idaho Statesman*, published daily out of Boise, that people across the Northwest were in awe of Nampa's treatment of its waste, and that the average daily flow handled by the plant was only half what it was technically capable of processing.

Groups of residents, tourists, and captive school children routinely toured the plant, one of Nampa's less than scenic attractions.

No shit.

Left to Write

I often think of writing as poking a few small holes in my swollen brain to release tension, allowing some pressing ideas to escape and make their way into print.

I began writing as an anxious youngster partly as relief, and also because my voice was so weak, I grew weary of having to state everything twice.

I grew weary of having to state everything twice.

Subconsciously, I think I figured I might as well try to develop a strong story-telling voice; maybe then people would really pay attention to me and listen.

Other than childhood poems, thank you notes after Christmas and birthdays, and mandatory school papers answering questions like "Why God Made Me" or "How Caterpillars become Butterflies," the only writing I did on a regular basis was as a child in my diary. Later, I referred to this daily account of my nerve-wracking life as my journal, to sound more grown up and sophisticated.

A vivid writing memory goes back to sixth grade at St. Paul's School in Nampa, Idaho, when Sister Hildegard, "Sister Mary Scary" as we called her, was my teacher. Not only was she shriveled-up old and with a strong resemblance to the Wicked Witch of the West, she was also lacking in teaching skills, or so many of us believed.

I should add that she was also lacking in basic, common sense. Take the day she announced to our class after lunch, "You know folks, I have been dead before."

Twenty-three mouths fell open.

"The Lord took me while I was on the operating table having my gall bladder removed a few years ago, and I saw Him. But miraculously, part way through the procedure he changed his mind about my destiny, and I came back to life.

"Now, put your heads down on your desks and thank Him that he spared me, in order to guide all of you to Him."

One afternoon not long after that episode, during a vicious spring thunderstorm I grew bored as Sister Scary prattled on about God cursing the earth with lightning and thunder, punishing us for our sins. Each time a boom of thunder, followed by a blast of lightning rocked the skies overhead, Sister would command us in her crackling, over-used voice, her hands wildly clapping.

"Boys and Girls! Bless yourselves with the sign of the cross, and thank the Lord you were not stricken by his rage!"

Trying hard not to allow this threatening nonsense to unnerve me, I doodled on a piece of notebook paper hidden under my catechism book. I had mastered my cursive years earlier, a victim of parochial school nuns' obsession with penmanship, neatness and Jesus.

Suddenly it occurred to me it might be a nice change to write backwards. I was somewhat impressed when I found this talent came naturally to me. Starting at the right margin and heading left, I could quickly form my letters backwards, without much effort at all. The end result was delightfully different, almost like a foreign language with a different set of letters than ours.

I was hooked.

Once certain I had mastered the technique, I cornered a like-minded friend in the girls' lavatory during recess time, where I shared my discovery. She was intrigued, and before long I had taught her to write in the opposite direction. Needing some diversion, and to share the latest gossip about our classmates, we began secretly exchanging notes written backwards.

For even more fun, we came up with the idea of reading the notes more quickly and efficiently; we brought compact mirrors to class. The good times lasted until one day Sister Scary found a crumpled-up note on the floor near my desk, slowly opened the note and looked perplexed, then irate.

"What is this gibberish? Who wrote this nonsense?" she bellowed, drawing the attention of most everyone in the class, all but the most distracted cases of ADHD, an affliction we didn't know much about back then.

When no one confessed, the mad nun strutted over to my desk, and I was sure I was a goner.

Leaning down to cackle into my trembling ear, she whispered, "My child, this rather looks like your handwriting to me."

Only backwards, I thought to myself. Good eye, Sister.

I chose not to respond but to study the inkwell on top of my desk while the nun rattled on.

"But I know you are not the type of girl to write something like this."

Smiling as big a grin as you ever got from the creature, she patted my spinning head and waddled back to her perch in front of the class.

At that moment, I realized my quiet voice and timid demeanor might not be a curse, but a gift.

If Sister Scary by any chance had a pet, it just might be me.

It was probably not until my senior year in high school that I fully realized my passion for writing. It was a bright, quirky English teacher named Gay Campbell who seemed to bring out the best in me. Reportedly Mrs. Campbell contacted my mother, wanting to share her excitement over my potential as a writer.

I have her to blame. Writing was obviously a tremendous help in college with all the required term papers, essays, and reports. Somehow I became known as a relatively prolific writer, and was often asked by friends to write papers in exchange for rewards like a pitcher of beer or a ride downtown. If I had the time and inclination, I might whip something off for a good friend, but I certainly didn't write for just anyone.

Once in graduate school at the University of Southern California, matters intensified. I barely had time to write my own papers let alone someone else's. Much of that anxious, tense time spent in Los Angeles is a blur now. I do recall many a night lying awake waiting for the ground to open up under my Murphy bed. I'd often arrive at class exhausted, not so much from cramming the night before, but due to lack of sleep as I waited for "The Big One," the quake predicted at any moment, the natural disaster that would leave the state of California at the bottom of the Pacific Ocean, while Nevada and Arizona would become coastal states.

It was while living in this perilous state that I recall experiencing my first full-blown anxiety attack. Today I would recognize my symptoms, but back then I was sure it was a major catastrophe, maybe a heart attack, or possibly a debilitating, early-onset stroke. Sudden death was always another possibility.

My first visual migraine would hit late in my first semester. While in the middle of my physiology final exam, a fuzzy line and flashing lights crossed the center of my paper. Naturally, I panicked. A brain tumor had always been one of my nagging worries and this was a sure sign. Somehow I managed to finish the test, feeling as though I were inebriated, writing under an intense strobe light without the disco music.

After class I paced the hallway waiting for the professor to gather her papers and exit the classroom, where I caught her. Describing what I tried to convince her was a rapidly growing brain tumor, she asked if my symptoms were still present.

"No, everything seems normal now, I just have a lingering,

dull headache and my head feels like a block of dead wood," I managed to reply.

"Nan, you have described what sounds precisely like a form of migraine which is accompanied by a visual aura. Go home, get a good night's rest, and drop by my office in the morning. In the meantime, I find little cause for much concern. And by the way, have you been under significant stress lately?"

I shot her a look as if to say, "Uh, nothing out of the ordinary. It is just that I am living alone on ground about to fall in the ocean, attending classes in one of the city's most crime-ridden neighborhoods, and slowly killing myself to earn a master's degree with honors. Not to mention the hellish traffic I battle to get from here to there while trying to survive on a few dollars a day."

Instead I mumbled something about learning to relax, thanked her and hurried off to my car, praying it had not been vandalized again by yet another desperate hoodlum lurking around the outskirts of our idyllic campus.

The House Dressing

Mildred C. Look was a sixties fashion designer who lived on a farm in Idaho with her peacocks, sheep and husband, Elmer, until her death in 1973.

Aunt Millie, as I knew my Grandma Kilmer's older sister, received little recognition for her ground-breaking work in couture. Though her designs were carefully sewn and intricately detailed, the models she dressed distinguished her creations; the woman designed and hand-stitched an elaborate wardrobe for her dish detergent bottles.

Millie was by no means a fashion plate herself. She normally greeted callers in a modest, faded, cotton housedress belted not so much to cinch her thick waist, rather, to hold up her immense, pendulous bosoms, or so it appeared to my five-year-old logic. In her cracked, black leather, lace-up shoes and shiny, "boldly beige" support hose, she hardly turned heads, but she looked great to me. Her generous mane of shiny silver and white hair was kneaded into a perfect bun, and her aqua eyes sparkled like prisms when she talked about things she loved, like crochet, rhubarb pie, and Jesus. She stood barely five feet tall, and while she slouched with age, I looked up to her.

Everything about this woman seemed honest and good, except her choice of husbands.

Uncle Elmer was creepy, I sensed early on, in part because Mommy never allowed me to sit on his lap, even though he often liked to pat his quads and try to lure me up there when we visited. Otherwise, I didn't pay much attention to the old codger.

Millie's world was different from mine or any I'd seen on TV sitcoms like *Leave it to Beaver*, *Father Knows Best*, *Donna Reed*, or my favorite, *The Dick Van Dyke Show*. My own life seemed lacking in glamour and excitement compared to those perfect television families. I'd lie in bed at night developing plots for my own dramas, often casting Mary Tyler Moore as my mother, with Dick Van Dyke as Dad. My stories never took place in Idaho; rather, they'd develop in exotic locales like Beverly Hills and New York City, which at the time I knew through television and the few movies I'd seen at the local theater.

Growing up, Sunday afternoons often meant piling into our Station Wagon to head out to tiny Wilder, Idaho to visit Millie and her menagerie. Not that our setting at home in Nampa was that bad, but I looked forward to escapes to my great aunt's farm some thirty minutes away. Hers was a one-story, wood framed farmhouse with peeling white paint, reminding me of Auntie Em's place in the scary *Wizard of Oz*, which I was forced to watch with the family each spring when it was televised. Weathered and dilapidated is how I'd describe the place today.

The house faced the main road, and around back the squeaky screened door opened to a long porch sprawled along the edge of the barnyard, where we'd often find Millie rocking in her chair as we drove into the barnyard. While snapping green beans, stitching a garment, or reading scripture, she kept watch over her property.

It was not so much the house, but its stuffing that intrigued me. Auntie Millie, with her staunch faith in Jesus, seemed not to believe in trash. Her home was so bloated with old magazines like *Look*, *Life*, *Readers' Digest*, *The Herald Christian*, *Family Circle*, *The Saturday Evening Post*, newspapers, letters, greeting cards, rubber bands, paper bags, cans and boxes, that there were no hallways, only paths.

Millie's "coverlets" amused me most. She left nothing naked. Hers was the cluttered, damp washroom where I first encountered a rather large, plastic, acrylic-haired doll perched on the back of the toilet. Her generously lashed eyes blinked at me from under a wide-brimmed, miniature straw hat. The doll's cascading pink skirt of yarn was designed to discreetly conceal the toilet tissue. Millie crocheted, knit and sewed special covers for the coffee pot, toaster, iron, pressure cooker, telephone, adding machine, tissue boxes, phone book, Bible, toothpick dispenser, salt and pepper shakers, anything in the house with more than two dimensions.

But my favorite was the attire she created for her detergent bottles. My great aunt intricately hand sewed with gingham, dotted Swiss, lace and ribbon, an entire wardrobe for her "Joy."

The white, plastic cap served as the head of Joy's voluptuous figure, and sensible, yet fashionable dresses fit snuggly over the otherwise nude bottle. The effect was quite flattering.

Each visit, I eagerly plowed my way through the maze of junk over to Millie's kitchen sink, where I'd check out the outfit her detergent was wearing that day.

Many an afternoon I'd perch atop Millie's kitchen stool, watching as she prepared one of her specialties, like lamb-burger casserole laced with black walnuts from her trees outside, roasted squirrel kabob, or lumpy green tomato cobbler I more than once mistook for apple, much to my disappointment. Most ingredients were grown or raised on her farm, and she was proud of her ingenuity in the kitchen. She liked to teach me as she hammered away at a stringy flank steak or pinched a powdery pie crust. Things like, "never salt your meats before you cook them; salt robs the flesh of its natural moisture." Or "pop your piecrust into the oven for five minutes before you add your filling. That way you'll never suffer a soggy crust under your favorite pie."

Her life lessons were not always related to food. Before a visit one day, Mother had woven my long hair into French braids, so I could not wait to show Aunt Millie my new "do." Arriving at the farm, I dashed into the house, nearly knocking over a three-foot high pile of old newspapers, and tripping over a half dead plant plopped in the middle of the kitchen floor.

"Aunt Millie!" I shrieked. "Look at me, don't I look cute?"

She looked at me with an expression hard to read, stooping to look into my eyes, then gently tugged at one of my prized pigtails.

"Little Nanner, of course you look precious, but that is for others to comment. You must never compliment yourself, as that would be boasting. The good Lord frowns upon vanity."

At five, I made a mental note. I'd wait for someone else to toot my horn, and often that was Millie.

Or maybe I could write a book . . .

From an early age, I sensed that my great aunt could keep a secret, so sometimes I shared pages of my carefully guarded diary. She liked hearing my poems, so I'd read to her when we were alone:

"TO BE"

I'd like to be my cat
Lying in the sun
I'd hope to be my dog
Sneaking a morning run
I'd not want to be a parent
With a child who's gone missing
I'd hate to be myself
With no one else to listen
I'd like to be the moon
Brightening a darkened sky
I'd love to be myself
If only I could fly.

As I matured, Millie and I talked about deeper things I did not share with my mom or friends, as they just wouldn't get it. Like how I always felt different. I did not mind telling my great aunt, as I knew she would understand, or at least pretend she did. And she'd always come up with just the right thing to say to me to make me feel okay about myself.

Take the afternoon I was confiding in her while we shelled walnuts, and she consoled me.

"You, my dear, are a special child. The good Lord has blessed you with a bright mind and sensitive heart, so you will understand and feel more than the average person, trust me. You must be brave, little lady. And everything will be all right." Then she gave me one of her big, smothering hugs, swatted me on my bottom, and sent me off to play.

While the family fingered through her endless stacks of old magazines, took turns pumping the worn pedals of Elmer's antique organ, or hollered at the old black and white Quasar TV set blasting the afternoon football game, I crept about the house. Quietly, I poked my way through the piles of Millie's life, delighting in the eccentricity of it all.

Rummaging through the old farmhouse was a treat, but after a few hours the clutter, chatter, and closeness began to suffocate. I took refuge outside, wandering the grounds girdling their bulging home, constantly on the lookout for those terrifying peacocks.

A favorite pastime was climbing to the top of the neatly-stacked bales of hay, then daringly leaping into the crunchy bundles of straw. For those few, heavenly moments in the air—I was flying!

Those were rich afternoons I spent scavenging black walnuts, pestering the dumb sheep, and snatching up wild flowers for Millie's supper table. My time outdoors was best spent exploring the weathered old barns and haylofts scattered about the farm. One particular day I came upon a box full of strange little pieces of wood, the likes of which I had never seen, half hidden on a shelf in the barn. I called upon my brother Biff to come out and examine the oddities.

"Uh, Nance, I don't think this is the kind of thing a little girl needs to look at—let's put these away and never mention it to anyone, okay?—especially not Aunt Millie."

Many years later Biff confided in me that these were Uncle Elmer's "butt rings," at which point I told him I wanted to hear nothing more about the subject.

Meanwhile, it seemed like no one ever knew, or cared where Elmer might be. He raised sheep on their land and was quite successful, we only found out after he was dead. The couple produced no children, some say this was on account of Millie's insistence on separate bedrooms. Others claimed she was simply not fertile. I tend to think she didn't care all that much for the man she married for some reason or another.

I heard some whispering over the years about how Elmer was not above "entertaining" the wives of some of his farm hands right there in the back of the house, while Millie hosted Bible study groups in the front parlor. I could only guess what this involved but it sounded sinister to my naïve ears.

The author, age 1, sitting on Grandma Hazel's lap, with Aunt Millie, Uncle Elmer, and her great Grandma Crowe.

At any rate, it was not until Millie succeeded Elmer in death and, much to the family's dismay, willed her small fortune to the Seventh Day Adventist Church, that we realized just how well old Uncle Elmer had done with his sheep.

Despite Elmer and the peacocks, the Looks' farm set the scene for some magical childhood adventures. To this day, I can't look at a bare detergent bottle without blushing, on account of my more than Great Aunt Millie.

Like Butter

According to the Roman Catholic Church, children are not capable of committing sin until the completion of their seventh year, when they have reached the "age of reason" and can decipher right from wrong. Until then youngsters are considered "innocents."

Call me precocious, but on the brink of five I knew darn well I should not be sneaking into our neighbor's kitchen to swipe a finger full of butter. This was downright wrong, but some days I couldn't resist. Tempting as gold, the pale yellow log sprawled across its dish, basking atop the shiny, Formica table. The thrill wasn't simply the salty cream sliding down my throat, but the prickly sensation of getting in and out of the house undetected, like some preschool cat burglar.

It was the late 1950s and the butter versus margarine controversy rattled the country. While I adored the taste of real butter, my mother insisted margarine was a better choice. Not only was it a healthier spread, she claimed, it was cheaper, a major draw for a family with four growing kids. Feeling deprived, I soon discovered that our next door neighbors the Gratins, a middle-aged spinster and her shriveled-up mother, still indulged in Darigold, the real thing. What's more, they kept it out in plain sight on their kitchen table.

It was not unusual for the younger Miss Gratin to call to me from their back porch when she'd spot me on the swing set in our yard, inviting me in for a cookie, marshmallow or whatever bait she might have on hand. I was normally willing to visit, though she never offered what I craved. Recognizing butter as not a proper snack, I didn't dare ask for a small bowl of it or even a quick few spoonfuls.

In a weaker moment and uninvited, I might sneak over to peek through the Gratin's back screen door. Across their tiny kitchen I could see through to the front living room, where the two women often watched daytime television programs like *As the World Turns* and the *Art Linkletter* show. I wondered why the daughter often sat close to her mother squeezing the woman's skinny, wrinkled wrist while glancing down at her watch; it didn't seem like they were ever going anywhere.

Once certain the women were distracted, I'd sneak through the backdoor into the kitchen, head towards the table to gingerly lift the glass cover off the butter dish, and help myself to a delicious scoop. Within seconds I was out the door and back soaring in my swing, higher than ever.

For a long time I thought I had gotten away with this caper. Until I ran into the not so young Gratin daughter in church years later, who delighted in teasing me, "Oh, Nanner, my mama and I used to get such a kick out of watching you devour our butter when you were a little tyke!"

Undoubtedly red faced, I thought to myself, "I wish you had just put a stop to my antics back then, and detoured me en route to a life of sin, shame, and addiction."

About the time I was pilfering butter from the Gratin's kitchen, my grandparents from the east coast arrived by train to visit us in our little town of Nampa, Idaho. My abandoned grandmother had remarried a lovable fisherman from Virginia, and the saggy old couple, strangers to me, were given the upstairs bedroom my sister and I shared. Sis and I would sleep on an air mattress in my parents' room during that time, which was a novelty, so we didn't whine.

My curiosity got the better of me after a few days, when I woke from my nap one afternoon and found myself alone upstairs. I thought I heard my grandparents bickering from the first floor, so surmised I could do a little surveillance in my bedroom, now occupied by outsiders.

Tiptoeing in, I scanned the room and found several women's dresses, a man's dark suit and some shirts hanging in my closet, my own clothes shoved aside to make space for the invaders'. I also noticed a new smell, and scoured the room for the source. There, atop our dressing table, little bottles of some sort of potions posed, along with a round, pink box with a fluffy pad sitting on top. Creeping around the room at its edges to avoid the creaky center beams, I reached the table and snatched the fluffy pad. Instantly, a cloud of white powder poofed everywhere, and as I cleared my eyes, I felt a smack on my rear end.

"What is the little mouse into now?" Grandma hissed at me. "Sneaking around and getting into Grandma's things?"

Frankly, I was not only frightened, but annoyed. This was my space and I had every right to see what was going on anytime I felt like it. But I didn't dare say anything other than "I'm sorry Grandma," and scurried downstairs, leaving the annoying woman muttering to herself as she rearranged the toiletries on *my* vanity table.

Not much was said about the incident, but for the rest of their visit Grandma referred to me rather curtly as that "little mouse" which I interpreted as "dirty rat."

None too soon, I stood alongside my family, waving enthusiastically as the train pulled away from the station, transporting my grandparents back to where they belonged and me to a den of guilt and shame—even before I'd turned seven.

At four or five, my escapades might have been harmless, some might even say cute, but as I grew closer to the dreaded "Age of Reason," I continued my wayward behavior. Still believing I could get away with anything short of a bank robbery or murder, not that I ever wanted to hurt anyone, I continued my sneaky actions. So upon turning eight, I had overnight become a full blown sinner, someone who would go straight to hell should death come early, unless of course I could make it to confession before I croaked.

By that age, in third grade, my pranks required more complicated orchestration.

For special occasions, my mother often baked a delectable sheet cake brimming with banana, raisins, spices and walnuts, smothered in cream cheese frosting. This had to be my favorite dessert. One spring day just before the annual school picnic, for which my mother had baked her specialty, she artfully frosted the cake and left it on the kitchen counter to set. She then headed out the door to get her hair done, which I knew always gave me about two full hours of freedom to scavenge the house and do whatever I wanted. That day all I was compelled to do was dig into that cake, its irresistible aroma infiltrating the house.

Passing back and forth through the kitchen, pretending to ignore the temptation sitting on the counter, I suddenly lost control. I had to have a taste, so quickly devised a plan. I would skillfully slice the top off the cake, then cut a layer from the center, replace the top, and smooth the creamy frosting over the remaining, albeit shorter cake. I set to work, but was so eager I completely botched the undertaking, destroying the creation.

I had to think fast. Noticing one of our mischievous new Siamese kittens clawing at the drapes, everything fell into place. Without hesitation, I scooped up the larger of the two cats, lifted her into the air above the cake, and plopped the frightened ball of fur directly into the center. The frosted kitty fought a few moments to gain traction, then quickly leapt from the pile of sticky crumbs, licking her body parts until her fur glistened and was no longer tasty.

Mom was home on schedule, and as I detected her driving into the garage I had to decide whether to give her a heads up on what the pet had done, or let her discover it on her own. I went with informing her up front, and she was mad, but not as irate as I'd expected. Regardless, she bought the story of the cat bombing the cake, I did not get in trouble, and she baked another without question.

It bothered me watching Mom curse that "darn cat" for weeks and I felt guilty about my deceit, but not enough to deny myself two slices at the picnic. I could always ask Father Frank to get God to forgive me, next time our class went to confession. I'd have to downplay the incident, like it was just a silly prank, so he would not assign too much penance for my sins. Everyone knew the kids who knelt the longest at the front of the church after confession were the really bad sinners. Standard penance was three Our Fathers and the same number of Hail Marys while kneeling. One classmate, Duane Strong, spent what seemed like years at that altar rail. His criminal record included pulling down his pants to expose himself to Sister Clementine, setting fire to the incinerator on the playground, and attempting to derail a Union Pacific train chugging through town.

Perhaps this wayward lad's time at the altar was only the beginning of a life behind bars.

It is not like I was ever going to end up on *America's Most Wanted* or in some maximum security prison for women, but I did worry constantly about burning in hell if I did not change my ways.

Thanks in part to the fact that I got caught breaking the law in high school, I eventually decided to clean up my act.

In Idaho up until the 80s, a fourteen-year-old child could be issued a driver's license, given there were so many rural kids whose families needed help on the farm driving tractors and other farm equipment. However, to operate a vehicle after dusk, one had to be sixteen. For weeks before I turned that magical age, I planned a special celebration.

It so happened there was a high school basketball game that fateful night, and I invited my friend Jody for a sleepover at my house afterwards. At the stroke of midnight, we quietly stuffed our pillows under the covers of my double bed, giving the appearance, in dim light, of two bodies peacefully sleeping. Next, we snuck out the back door at the opposite end of the house from my parents' bedroom. Holding our breath, we opened the creaking garage door, and waited for any sound of life. The coast was clear. As planned, I took the driver's seat and put the car in neutral. Then, with Jody poised at the hood, she effortlessly pushed the little white VW bug down the driveway and into the street.

Silence.

I turned the key and before we knew it we were winding our way through the dark, deserted streets of Nampa. At the time, I was attending the Catholic high school twenty miles away in Boise, where most of my friends lived, including Jody. So we headed out to the freeway, en route to the state capital, where we'd arranged to pick up Cliff, my current boyfriend. The three of us would then drive around town for an hour or two, just because we could.

Cliff was waiting behind his garage, as instructed, and jumped into the back seat for a quick cruise around the neighborhood. Beaming with grown-up confidence, I noticed a red light flashing in my rearview mirror. I pointed out the squad car behind us, with little concern. After all, I was of age and we had done nothing wrong, as far as I knew.

I slowed the car and skillfully pulled to the side of the road, waiting for the husky cop to saunter up as I rolled down my window to chat.

“What are you young folks up to at this time of night?”

“Uh, we’re just driving around and talking,” I answered, trying to sound casual, yet mature.

“Lemme see your license, young lady,” were his next words.

Proudly pulling mine from the glove box, I pointed to my date of birth and waited as he shined his flashlight directly into my eyes, nearly blinding me, then down at my license, then back into my eyes.

“Haven’t you kids heard about curfew?”

“What curfew?” Jody innocently asked, leaning from the passenger seat.

“You kids oughta know there is a twelve a.m. curfew for anyone under eighteen, so I’m gonna have to take you all down to the station.”

My birthday wasn’t turning out as planned. Once at the station in downtown Boise, the officer phoned my dad at home in bed.

“Hello, yes, Mr. Kilmer, this is Officer Wright calling from the Boise Police Station, and we have your daughter and her friends down here. I picked them up for curfew violation about twenty minutes ago.”

Interrupting, and half asleep, my dad mumbled, “I am afraid there has been some mistake, my daughter is home asleep in her bed.”

Click, then dial tone.

Double checking the number then phoning our house again, the conversation was repeated, this time with a bit more force, convincing my dad to drive over to Boise in the middle of the night to rescue his delinquent daughter from the slammer.

Dad wasn’t that miffed about our little adventure but Mom was out of her mind and grounded me for a full month from everything but school, church, and my cheerleading duties. She quivers to this day when she tells people like my kids about her delinquent daughter’s “run-in with the law.”

Frankly I have always thought of my time spent in jail as a fairly positive experience. Not only did I realize that I *could*, and *would* get caught being sneaky, I wanted to believe the incident squelched my mother’s hopes I could ever become a beauty queen.

After all, who ever imagined a Miss America with a criminal record?

The Thinker

I had never thought much about the word "sneak" until I began teaching English to Japanese staff at the advertising agency in Tokyo where I was working as a copywriter. It was the mid-eighties and in addition to writing copy I was assigned the task of helping some of the firm's creative team to speak my language. I conducted small classes in a stuffy conference room during lunchtime.

Having no training in teaching language, I struggled to help my colleagues grasp sufficient knowledge of English to get by at meetings with Western clients, as they attempted to promote their creative concepts.

If nothing else, we had a good time. And I learned as much as they did as I attempted to explain expressions we native speakers take for granted like "the door is ajar," which brought puzzled looks to even the sharpest of my pupils.

One day I reprimanded a mischievous young man named Morimoto when he arrived late for class and tried to enter unnoticed.

"Trying to sneak in, Morimoto san?" I asked with a smirk.

"What *sneak* is, Nan san?" he inquired earnestly. I had to think a moment; sneak means . . . I tried to simplify my definition.

"Well, *sneak* means to go into the room without anyone knowing it."

"Is this bad?" the Japanese student innocently asked.

"Not really," I offered. "Sometimes *sneak* is good, like when you don't want the bad guy to see you. But sometimes it is bad, like when you are trying to rob a bank."

I was not sure I myself understood what I had said and am quite sure my student was confused.

That evening as I crammed myself into the overflowing subway car, I pondered the word sneak. Having been called one as a kid, I felt compelled to defend myself. A quiet child, I believed I was simply going about my business without being noticed. I was playing it safe. A kid never knew what might get her in trouble so it seemed wise to practice stealth. So this was not necessarily a bad trait, but one I found slightly thrilling and often very helpful in sticky situations.

Take playing over at my neighbor, Melody Rose's house, for instance. Her mother Dorothy might as well have ordered us to sneak around, she was so ridiculously strict. It was not unusual for me to visit "Melrose," as I liked to call my pal, after dinner in the summertime when I'd help her with the dishes. "Dot," her mom, did not like to use her new dishwasher for fear of water marks and smudges. So Melrose would wash and

I'd dry, while her mom and dad sat in the adjacent, tiny dining room sipping their after dinner coffee and discussing his next business trip. Mr. Hechinger, known around town as "Sonny," was a train conductor so was often on the road, or I should say, tracks.

Although Dot could not see us, she could hear everything we said, so we had to do a lot of mouthing of words. Melrose might tie her dish rag under her eyes like a bandit, or flip me in the rear end with a towel, sending us into silent convulsions. The worst was when we could no longer control our laughter, and together burst into hysteria.

"You girls stop being silly, or Nanner is going straight home!" Dot would scold us. "Now stop your nonsense!"

For some reason I could not comprehend, laughter was not allowed in the Hechinger household, so we had to be sneaky about our antics. Further perplexing to me was Dot's lighter, or maybe I should say perverse, side to her otherwise stern personality. Take the day she called me and Melrose into her bedroom, where she sat nude on her bed.

With her legs crossed, head slumped and right arm supporting her chin, she announced, "Look at me girls; I am *The Thinker*."

At the time we were amused and giggled uncontrollably, even though we knew we were breaking house rules. It was not until years later that I became acquainted with Rodin's famous statue, the one Mrs. Hechinger had been impersonating that day. I thought of Dot during my year abroad when I visited Paris and viewed the famous bronze statue in the *Musee Rodin*. Interestingly enough, the statue depicts a somber person deep in thought apparently struggling with some inner conflict. The man looks almost incapable of a smile let alone laughter.

Who knew Dot was cultured?

To justify my own conflicted feelings about the word *sneak*, I refer to several definitions from Merriam Webster:

—to go or move in a quiet, stealthy way

—to behave in a cowardly or servile way

—to creep or steal away privately

—to escape notice

I prefer the last to describe my behavior, naughty or nice.

After all, God is always watching.

The author and co-workers skiing in Japanese Alps, 1986.

Fallout

It didn't seem like long after the barnyard trauma at Aunt Millie's when I started hearing about some kind of "cold war" going on in our often scary world. I wondered if there were another kind of war, maybe a warmer one, and if that might be any less threatening. I was afraid to ask too many questions, for fear of what I might learn.

Every evening our family gathered around the Magnavox TV set to watch Walter Cronkite deliver the nightly news; his serious tone and deep voice frightened me. I learned that the Russians had something called missiles, not to be confused with our prayer books, lined up to shoot at us from somewhere down below Florida, where my Grandma and Grandpa Kilmer vacationed most winters. They were calling this problem "The Cuban Missile Crisis" and it seemed like it was all people talked about in those days.

I never wanted to plop directly in front of the television set, as I was scared to look directly at Mr. Cronkite. Instead I'd position myself and my toys off to the side of the room, where I could keep sight of him from the corner of my eye, and still hear whatever doom and gloom he'd have to deliver to the country that night.

Fiddling with my small, wooden dollhouse, I'd imagine the daily life of the miniature family dwelling inside as I rearranged the tiny furniture. There was a father, mother, brother, sister and neuter baby living inside the house. I'd often change the dynamics of what was going on in the family, always making sure the baby was safe and the father came home from work every night. Theirs was always a very happy, secure family with few problems other than maybe an overturned coffee table in the living room or a missing rung from the baby's crib.

I could not figure out why some evil people might be planning to bomb our country and kill us all, maybe themselves included. This seemed contradictory to everything I had learned about God and the Ten Commandments and treating others like you'd like them to treat you.

This Walter Cronkite guy always ended his thirty minutes of mostly bad news with the statement, "And that's the way it is, Monday, October 26th, 1962," or whatever gloomy day it might have been.

And I quickly tried to block the thought that October 27th might never come.

Infatuated with President Kennedy and his beautiful family, I had to believe he could save us all from destruction. I fantasized about being his daughter, Caroline, living in the White House with her two fabulous parents, and adorable baby brother, John-John.

I believed in President Kennedy almost more than in God. I hoped with his handsome looks and charm he could talk the Russians out of blowing up the world. I knew about war and that it was real, as my own father had fought in World War II when he was only seventeen, and I'd seen pictures of him in his uniform with a gun! My grandma told me he had fibbed about his age and claimed to be eighteen so he could fight for our country. He ended up flying bombers over North Africa and Italy, which thrills me to think about now. When he was alive, he did not speak much about his wartime experiences, but I imagine it must have been horrible, and my mother told me some of his fellow soldiers and friends died during that terrible time.

During that so called "Cuban Missile Crisis" I often had nightmares about looking up from the play yard and seeing hovering aircraft ready to drop huge bombs on our little town. Older kids in the neighborhood talked about bomb drills at their school. They had to hurry and hide under their desks when the alarm went off—like that might protect them from a nuclear bomb?

Luckily, President Kennedy was able to straighten out the tense situation and get the Russians to stop threatening our country, but folks were so shaken up that the talk of war and bombs continued, and people were assigned public shelters where they were to seek refuge in the event of a nuclear attack.

Other concerned citizens decided to take matters in their own hands and build their own, underground shelters. Mr. Hechinger was one such industrious person.

The Hechingers' house was not large by any means. There were three small bedrooms. Sonny and Dot's was in the front of the house, offering a bit of privacy with the bathroom separating theirs from the kids' rooms. Melody Rose and her older sister Sandy shared the middle room in the house, which was problematic not only because Sandy was ten years older and into boys and makeup while Melody Rose was still playing with dolls, but because their brother Clark, the middle child, had to pass through the girls' room to get to his own cramped bedroom in the back. The set up was far from ideal, but it was home.

Not long after the Cuban Crisis had subsided, Mr. Hechinger began carving out a cavity below their basement cellar. From the rickety back porch, warped wooden steps led down to the cellar, where clammy walls were lined up and down with Mason jars, all plump full of Dot Hechinger's jams, jellies, pickles, pears and peaches. Under this small tomb, Sonny painstakingly began digging out what could be called, with some exaggeration, a cavern, plastering the sides of the enormous hole with mushy cement until he'd created a ten-foot square hide-away, maybe eight feet below the main floor of his home.

Along with sixteen-year-old son Clark, Sonny was able to finish the entire project in less than three months. In the end it was no showplace, but perfectly comfortable and safe, he could only hope.

Before we knew it, Clark had taken over the shelter as his own, moving his belongings from the cramped back bedroom to the dungeon. He claimed it offered maximum privacy, and twenty-four hour darkness, for those luxurious weekends when he could sleep through the day. And although the walls bulged and buckled here and there, by the dim light of the battery-powered lanterns scattered about the cubicle, no one would notice.

"Man, I dig my new underground pad," Clark used to crack about his new quarters far from the rest of the family. Here no one bothered him as he plugged away at his guitar or blasted rock and roll. Deep under the house, his bellowing music no longer set off Sonny's temper, blurred the television screen or vibrated the rafters.

The Hechingers' underground addition, in a real sense, offered much more than respite from an atomic attack. The bomb shelter was Clark's refuge.

Around the same time bombs threatened and shelters were dug and President Kennedy was killed and there was almost more than we could all handle, a woman went missing in Nampa.

Lillian Richey lived not far from the high school, in a small tract house in a typical Nampa neighborhood. Lillian's husband had passed away several years earlier, and her grown son was living out of town somewhere.

I don't know a lot about this mystery because the matter was kept rather hush-hush, as this type of thing just didn't happen in Nampa in those days. Reportedly, one night Lillian came home from a date, put her purse on the kitchen table, took off her coat, hung it on the chair, and disappeared, never to be seen again.

Stories festered.

She'd perhaps willingly run off with her date, left town and was beginning an exotic new life in South America, or possibly some remote island in the South Pacific. Maybe her only child had her murdered in quest of his inheritance. Investigators did not rule out the possibility that her husband was secretly still alive and the two had run off together to make the most of his life insurance money.

The Medical Center theory caught my attention. At the time, a fancy new health care facility was being built around the corner from the Richey's house, and the night of Lillian's disappearance the site was no more than a huge, gaping hole in the ground. Speculation began as to Lillian's body being dumped in the vast pit, covered over with dirt, and "laid to rest" beneath the future Mercy Medical Center.

By the time a group of Nampa's sharpest homicide detectives came up with the idea that Mrs. Richey's body might have been dumped under the foundation of the Medical Center, construction had already progressed to the first floor of the proposed three- story building.

Rumbling bulldozers were promptly ordered onto the lot, and excavation began at the site in an attempt to locate the missing person.

A body was never found beneath Mercy Medical Center.

Melody Rose and I spent hours riding our bikes past Lillian's house, the Medical Center construction site, the police station, the high school; wherever we thought we might find clues to this fascinating mystery.

One rainy, dreary afternoon we were sitting around the Hechingers' damp cellar, bored with Yahtzee, Checkers, and Gin Rummy, looking for something fun to do. With everything going on in our world, we'd become too scared to drag out the old Ouija board we'd so loved as younger innocents. Aware that Clark was away on a camping trip, we crept down to his cave. It was spooky, but we loved looking through his *Mad* magazines, girlie photos and poultry wishbone collection. Taking it all in, we gasped as we both looked up at the same time, noticing two softball-sized mounds, side-by-side and a few inches apart, protruding from the wall above her brother's dresser. Trembling, we traced with our fingertips what we fantasized to be Lillian's voluptuous breasts.

Bill Augsburger
Chief of Police

211 12th Avenue South
Nampa, Idaho 83651
(208)465-2257

NAMPA POLICE DEPARTMENT

MISSING PERSON

DATE REPORTED MISSING: February 10, 1964

Lillian Richey

Richey was approximately 51 years old. She was last seen at the Ranch Club in Garden City. She resided in Nampa. Lillian Richey was supposed to report to work at 12:00 PM at Bullock Jewelry Store in downtown Nampa. Lillian Richey lived alone at 336 W. Sherman. Her car was still at the residence. A white sport coat had been removed from the residence.

Lillian RIchey was described as 5-2, 115 to 120 pounds, blond hair and blue eyes. Lillian Richey was last seen at the Ranch Club in Garden City on Saturday night. Richey was driven home that night. Richey was supposed to have breakfast at 11 AM on Sunday. When her friends showed up on Sunday, Richey was not home. Richey has not been seen since.

Troubled Waters

Despite having grown up near the beach in Atlantic City, our otherwise buoyant mother never learned to swim. Determined to drown-proof her four kids, Mom enrolled each of us in swim lessons before we could even tie our own shoes. So I spent much of my childhood either fretting about water or submerged in it.

Oh, how I dreaded those soggy, scary classes. It didn't help that the summer before I was first subjected to the torture sessions, our family was vacationing at the lake when I tumbled out of our canoe into the deep, dark waters below. Dad, a state champion swimmer and diver, decided it best not to scoop me up out of the water until I had a chance to try to save myself.

I naturally panicked and sunk what seemed like a mile down under before Dad scooped me up with one arm, calmly reassuring me.

"It's OKAY, Nanner Poo. The water is our friend; it would have pulled you right back to the surface, even without my help. You need swimming lessons. Before you know it you'll be a champ like your pop."

I wanted to believe his promising words, but when that day arrived and I had to sit on the clammy turquoise bank of the HUGE municipal swimming pool waiting for our class to begin, I gagged, trying not to lose my breakfast. This was terrifying for a five-year-old land lover.

I somehow mastered the bobbing and bubble blowing required of "Tadpoles" and as a result was promoted to the status of "Mighty Minnow." I knew this meant the following summer I would be forced to willingly leap into deep water, then frantically paddle like a dog to the side of the pool—and safety. I spent the entire school year alternating between worrying about everything from a bomb dropping on Nampa, to a bird flying into my bedroom, to having to leap the following summer into that humongous concrete abyss known as Lakeview Pool. There, I might be sucked into oblivion.

"Mighty Minnows" was somehow passable for me so I was promoted to the more mature sounding "Advanced Beginner" class. At this point I began to overcome my paralyzing fear of water. That is, until a year later when I encountered the next daunting challenge. By then over four feet tall, I was able to maneuver a belly flop into six feet of water and dart like a frog back to the safety of the ledge. I could also hold my head underwater to the count of twenty-something and kick my feet like an outboard motor for what seemed like hours each morning while holding on to the side of the pool.

Gaining confidence, it was the following summer in my "Intermediate" class, when I was presented with the most daunting challenge of my swim career. At this point it was not so much about what I was able to do in the water, it was what had to happen from high above it that completely unnerved me. A requirement for passing this Red Cross class was a solo jump from the three-meter diving board.

Believing she was helping prepare me for what I considered to be an Evil Knievil-ish act minus the motorcycle, my mother had been chattering for weeks about the incomparable thrill of a high dive. Although the woman had never even put her face under water, she could barely contain herself at the thought of her little girl plummeting to the depths of the pool. Dad had taken time off from work to watch my performance, and Mom stood by with the Brownie camera, ready to capture the unforgettable moment on film. So there was no way I could turn back once I had climbed what seemed like a mile to the board at the top of the ladder. Without looking down or breathing, I inched my way to the end of the long, bouncy, plank which felt like sandpaper to my bare feet. I whispered a prayer to the Blessed Mother, who I was thinking would be more sympathetic in this situation than God or Jesus.

"Please, Mother of God, help me survive this plunge into hell."

Somehow I managed to force myself to take one final step off the board, out into roughly ten seconds of terror. Once I had crashed into the water and my feet hit the algae-covered bottom, I instinctively propelled myself up to the surface of the pool. Sputtering to catch my breath, I paddled to the nearest ladder and popped out of the pool where my parents and bystanders were still cheering with gusto. Mom was winding her camera for another shot of my victorious plunge and Dad beamed as he held open a plush pink towel, ready to wrap me up like a prize.

Growing up, with swimming almost as crucial for us Kilmers as attending mass on Sundays or maintaining straight A's, it was no surprise my first job landed me in the water. At fourteen I began teaching Nampa youngsters how to enjoy the water, or to at least keep themselves from a horrible, tragic death by drowning.

For a few years I was employed by the city as a "Tadpole Tykes" instructor and enjoyed trying to convince five and six year olds that the water was their friend. Of course some took to the pool more quickly than others, but more often than not I succeeded in convincing a scared kid to put their face in the water. If even for a second, this meant progress for both of us.

While in high school and college I followed in my older sister's footsteps and became a lifeguard each summer at Nampa's version of a country club. During off hours when the pool was closed, I conducted private lessons for members' kids, which made for very long days but a respectable bank account.

Swim Instructor/Lifeguard did not cover all my duties at the club. I also did babysitting, counseling, and maintenance work. It was not uncommon for presumptuous parents to dump their young kids with me while they played a quick nine holes or knocked back a few drinks at the "nineteenth hole." The worst was trying to deal with tipsy moms swaying out of the clubhouse hours later to retrieve their water-logged kids.

Lindy, a chubby woman better suited for a one-piece than the skimpy bikini she liked to wear, seemed particularly needy. She hung around the pool most days, her three unruly kids crawling over her body as she attempted to sunbathe, dumping ice cream in her lap and slapping each other until she'd order them back into the pool. Poor Lindy had discovered her husband had "other interests" which explained why he was never around. I tried to assure the struggling woman she was not alone; other weepy wives around the pool confided in me with similar woes. Trying to come across as a mature teen, I listened patiently and offered my sympathy, but seriously doubt I saved any marriages.

That was certainly not my job.

Along with the challenges of dealing with the clientele, I was responsible for keeping a sparkling pool, clean showers and toilets and a safe, tidy deck. My only diversion was watching many a duffer tee off on the nearby fairway, or joking around with the cute caddy boys hanging around the pro shop next door.

Regardless, the role of lifeguard was far from a breeze. The thought of being responsible for someone else's life is a petrifying burden. I have had recurrent nightmares over the years of arriving at the pool in the morning, and as I begin to vacuum the bottom, I notice three or four babies staring up at me from the bottom of the deep end—dead.

Just the Right Leg

For an unremarkable little town, Nampa had its share of interesting characters, aside from those already mentioned. Actually, for a town of less than twenty thousand, we might have had more than our share of eccentrics.

The Awker family lived three doors down from us, in a tiny, red brick house I always found a bit deceiving. It was frankly a rather ordinary-looking home when you considered the fabulous family living inside.

There was Harriet, the mother, originally from San Francisco. She was so sophisticated and worldly, unlike most of the other mothers in town. Her hair was silver, which made her look regal, not old, and she dangled professionally manicured nails. She was married to Peter Awker, a farmer who left each morning in his black Ford pickup truck, returning by sunset in his dirty overalls and rolled-up shirt sleeves.

I had a hard time accepting the fact that the head of this idyllic household, the husband of the perfect woman, and father of three stellar children, was a simple farmer who spent his days in muddy fields of alfalfa and corn.

I did not allow myself to think much about Mr. Awker back then. In the end, which came early for poor Mr. Awker when he was barely fifty years old, it seemed his liver could not keep up his liquor intake. Not that I blamed him. None of his family seemed to pay much attention to him as far as I could tell, and more often than not, he'd be whittling alone on his front porch with a tumbler by his side, as I'd peddle past on my bike some nights before dark.

"God rest his soul," Mom always petitioned whenever she mentioned dead people she had known if not loved.

Harriet was the first woman I knew who owned a genuine fur coat; a three-quarter length mink. She wore it each winter to mass on Sundays, bridge club once a week, occasional dinners out with Mr. Awker at the new country club, and the annual Christmas party at the downtown Elk's Club. She may as well have been a movie star, as far as I was concerned.

Willie was Harriet's youngest child and one of my best pals, a skinny kid with a crew cut and crooked smile. Willie and I seemed to harbor the same sense about life, and I always suspected he and I shared similar dreams of flying, though I don't recall ever talking about them.

I can see myself scampering about frantically when I'd spot Willie peddling up our front walk on his shiny, green ten-speed Schwinn.

Everything had to be just so for an Awker's visit. So I'd quickly stash all the family room clutter under the sofa, close off the kitchen with its sink full of dirty dishes, and adjust my braids in the foyer mirror.

Of course, Willie's house was always in perfect order, or so I believed.

One of Willie's older sisters, Marie, was the middle child. I mostly remember her long, auburn hair, slender figure, and the fact that she refused to wear any clothes from *Sears Roebuck*, which puzzled me for a while as my mother sewed most of our clothes, and the rest usually came from the *Sears* catalogue.

Later, I realized that Marie Awker might have been one of the first snobs I'd met.

The girl always seemed to be entertaining boys in the Awkers' lovely living room. I do not mean like Uncle Elmer entertained those farm hands' wives, but she obviously enjoyed the company of boys.

That front room was a better indication of the family than the exterior of the home. Elegant antiques from Europe, white overstuffed sofas, jewel-toned oriental rugs, and real, live flowers in crystal vases.

I saw similar rooms in the dental office issues of *House Beautiful and Better Homes and Gardens*, which I perused half-heartedly as I waited in terror to be summoned to Dr. Norton's chair in the dentist's office.

Then there was Claire, the oldest daughter, a prodigious pianist, over-achieving student, less glamorous than her younger sister Marie. Claire was stricken with bone cancer at the age of twelve; oh my gosh, I found this so excitingly dramatic, like something out of a television show. What's more, she and her mother actually flew off to Europe after the surgeon had removed her right leg, just above the knee. They visited Lourdes in southwestern France, the sacred sight of incredible, miraculous events, according to religious experts.

Reportedly, flocks of Christian pilgrims travel from all over the world to visit this sacred shrine in Lourdes where Saint Bernadette encountered the Virgin Mary in 1858. Many have sworn to be cured after drinking or bathing in the water in this mountain grotto at the foot of the Pyrenees in France.

Parishioners at our church, Saint Paul's, believed Claire would never have lived as long as she had, had she not journeyed to that holy sight. After all, she not only lost a leg, but a lung as well, when her doctors found the vicious cancer had spread.

Over the years, I have kept this profound story in mind, should the need for supernatural healing strike. If one of the most perfect girls I knew on this earth could suddenly be stricken with such a horrible disease, what might possibly happen to me?

It was comforting for me to know that outside of Nampa, somewhere out there—miracles happened.

I vividly remember poring over the Awker's photos of their European mission; they even saw Pope John XXIII in Rome. They brought home fashion magazines from Paris—*Marie Claire*, *Printemps* and *Jolie*—and the latest from France for hair styling, the "roller."

But as a wide eyed, precocious seven-year-old, my most captivating memory is of a particular drive I took over to Boise with Claire and Mrs. Awker about a year after they had returned from Europe. Claire needed a new leg, and Harriet had invited me to join her and her daughter on their special shopping trip.

I was forced to plead with my mother.

"Please oh please oh please let me let me go, Mommy; I want to go so badly!"

"I cannot for the life of me understand why you'd want to go with them, Nanner," she barked. "It sounds like the most depressing outing I've ever heard of. But go if you must; wear something nice, and let me curl your hair."

Mrs. Awker drove the three of us over in her new white, Pontiac Bonneville sedan with beige leather seats, air conditioning, and push-button windows.

The car had been a surprise for Mrs. Awker a few months earlier. One sparkling afternoon, Mr. Awker purchased the car at Honstead Motors in downtown Nampa, and he and Willie proudly stopped by to give me and my sister Debby a quick test ride.

Naturally, we youngsters could not resist poking at the tempting little silver buttons strategically positioned along the arm rests of each of the car's four doors, buzzing the windows up and down like a yo-yo.

At which point, by then cranky Mr. Awker lectured in his deep, monotone voice, "You know, kids, these windows are only going to go up and down so many times, and then they won't. Now cut it out!"

That was all he grumbled, but the fun was over unless we could come up with a good reason to open our window, which was not easy with the car being air-conditioned and all.

I recognize now that a pessimistic outlook on life might have contributed to Peter Awker's early death, along with liquor, loneliness and maybe some pesticides he used on his farm.

My special shopping trip with the Awkers took about thirty minutes on the old Highway. Boise was a hub for big city shopping, and Claire was looking specifically for a new right leg. She had shot up over two inches the previous year, so had outgrown her former limb, which had thrown off her gait. Purchasing a new leg at Southwest Idaho Prosthesis was truly one-stop shopping.

We arrived and Claire and her mother were escorted into the back room, where she would have her fitting. I waited outside, not by choice, but could easily hear every word being spoken, and could keep an eye on the feet of the fitting woman and Mrs. Awker, and on Claire's one foot.

I sat on the hard, cold, metal folding chair in the dimly lit hallway, and leaned way over, pretending to adjust the strap on my black, patent leather church shoes, which I had chosen for this special outing. That way, I could actually spy on the threesome (from their thighs down) as the woman carefully measured Claire's good and only leg, her foot, and her waist, as the fake leg would actually be attached to a belt.

Mrs. Awker spoke soothingly to her daughter, trying as she did to keep the mood in the cubicle as upbeat as possible.

"Oh my goodness, Claire, you are getting so tall! I envy you. Here I am barely five feet four, and you are already five-six and still growing," Mrs. Awker bubbled.

"Do you think I will have to get another new leg before I stop growing, Mother?"

"Don't worry, honey, it is no problem if you do. Our insurance covers most of the expense, and they are coming up with better and more attractive prosthetics all the time. Why, by the time you are a grown woman they will probably have such life-like legs no one will even realize yours in not real!"

"Oh, Mother, I hope you are right! And, ma'am, can you tighten the belt a little? It feels loose," Claire requested.

I remember wondering if she liked her job, that arm and leg fitting woman. At the time, I thought it seemed a little weird and scary. Today as an adult, I'd guess she might grow depressed after a while dealing with all those deformed bodies.

Once the measurements were all precisely recorded on a spiral notepad, aesthetics could be considered, like complexion, shape, markings, "muscle" tone, etc. After what seemed like hours to me, Claire's order was completed for a new plastic right leg, from which extended a fake woman's foot, the same size as Claire's only foot.

What's more, I overheard that Claire would be purchasing not one but two new right legs. One would be in a paler skin tone for use during the fall and winter months, then when spring came, she'd switch to a golden-tinted plastic limb to match her left, lightly tanned leg.

The next item on the shopping list that afternoon was shoes. Chances are you have never stopped to think about the new shoe dilemma for those unfortunate enough to have lost a leg at such a delicate age that the remaining leg's foot is still growing.

The *real* foot grows in short spurts late at night while you sleep, if one subscribes to the latest scientific research on growth patterns in children. Then you have the artificial foot on the fake leg. Do you buy a new leg every time your own, growing foot needs a new shoe? So that the fake foot keeps up in size with the natural one and so you can wear two of the same-sized shoes?

This is a puzzler. Our visit to the limb factory shoe room intrigued me, to say the least. I marveled at the selection of colors and styles, but to this day have not figured out the logistics of buying shoes for a pair of feet, only one of which grows.

Next came the most amazing part of the trip, the actual tour of the limb room. I will never forget the brightly lit, high-ceilinged, grayish-white chamber with no windows. Eerie dreams of this surrealistic space resurface now and then.

Bright, fluorescent lights buzzed softly overhead, illuminating the shiny body parts dangling from the ceiling, which ranged from muscular and deeply tanned, to scrawny and porcelain white. It seemed like any combination could be made available. I was most intrigued not by the variety of plastic legs and arms swaying from the iron rods overhead, but by the serene artists sitting below hunched over stark, wooden tables.

Tonight, as I recall this scene, I want to say soft, classical music was playing in the background.

These skilled craftsmen delicately painted on the prostheses moles of various shapes and colors, tiny, bluish spider veins, and assorted blemishes, all in a somewhat futile attempt to make them look more natural.

Driving home that dream-like day, I sat alone in the spacious, leather-lined back seat, staring at the backs of Claire's and her mom's carefully coiffed heads, thinking how their perfect lives had been scarred forever. It had all happened so quickly and again I thought to myself, "If tragedy could happen to an Awker, what might happen to me?"

My mind raced as I considered the dreadful possibilities, picturing myself a pathetic teenager paralyzed from the neck down after some freak, unpredictable accident. Or slumped motionless in a wheelchair, or perhaps legally blind, fumbling around the school hallways desperately trying to reach the right classroom.

Countless years later, I occasionally find myself thinking of Claire Awker as I notice a suspicious new mole or surfacing vessel—on my once flawless legs.

Miss Nothing

Somehow I knew I'd never be crowned Miss America. This being my mother's dream during my promising early years, I played along. Tucked in bed at night, I'd shiver as I pictured myself wobbling down the runway in a bathing suit and high heels, a "*Miss Idaho*" banner draped across my thickening torso. Considered pretty or not, I'd been in the Convention Center in Atlantic City, and could never place myself center stage there, or anywhere for that matter.

Until I was old enough to know better, I faithfully watched the Miss America Pageant on television each September. Not only because I tend to admire attractive, talented, seemingly confident people, but because my mother, having grown up in Atlantic City, had a vested interest in the contest. Thus she began grooming me early on, in hopes of having me crowned "Miss America" circa 1978. The sappy tune "There She is . . . our Ideal" festered in my head.

Despite my reluctance to compete in a beauty pageant, I refused to douse my mother's hopes. I stood tall when she poked me between my shoulder blades while waiting in line for Sunday communion, and I dutifully sat at the piano most afternoons, hitting the wrong note more often than not. Determined, Mom signed me up for dance lessons, where I proved more sure-footed and my talent for the contest was established. Tap, ballet, interpretive, modern, jazz, you name it—I was a star at the annual spring recital held in the Central Junior High gymnasium. Most years I threw up in the bathroom stall after each number, but Mom's beaming smile made me forget the jitters, nausea and vomit by the end of the show.

By the time I was pushing twelve, I'd begun acquiring a few too many pounds, creating doubt and dismay. I could still fit into a bathing suit, but only under a blousy cover-up. Mortified as I was to be considered chubby, at least I had a solid excuse. Who ever saw a plump beauty queen? Or worse, imagine a plump beauty queen dancing?

Alone in my room at night, I drew up mental lists of alternative goals and suitable careers. By focusing on a definite, plausible future, I believed I could ease my relentless anxiety about life and its uncertainties. For a time I tossed around the idea of composing clever, poignant, touching lines for a greeting card company, maybe even Hallmark.

Sharing my bright idea with my older, supposedly wiser sister Debby, she quipped,

"That is the dumbest job I ever heard of in my life!"

Crushed, I announced to myself, "Scratch that idea, idiot!"

For a while I was intrigued with the work of a pathologist, like I'd seen on *Columbo* during one of his wacky investigations.

My mother caught wind of this and scolded me, "Stop being so morbid! Who in the world would want to dissect dead bodies?"

Biff, my older brother and undependable hero, suggested I might fly as a stewardess, but I informed him it would make me a jittery mess serving hot coffee, tea, or me, in an often turbulent environment.

Restless, I tried to convince myself not to worry about eating myself out of the pageant and disappointing my mother or choosing the wrong career. After all, I was twelve and there was time before I had to confront such profound issues. I noticed my classmates did not seem bothered, and decided I was simply more advanced in my thinking and would try to guide those thoughts in a more positive direction. It was all I could control at the time; my weight had taken off on its own.

Thus began my religious phase when I'd slip off the playground and into the church during recess, where at the altar rail I'd kneel, staring up at the porcelain Virgin Mary posed in her alcove.

"If you care a lick about me, Mother of God, just give me one little sign," I'd plea. Then I'd imagine the stone carving winking at me ever so subtly, assuring me.

"Everything will be OK, Nanner. Just stop worrying and keep saying your daily prayers."

The author, age 5, as kindergarten graduate/aspiring beauty queen.

An Imperfect Pair

Say what you will about the Crowe sisters, but the two displayed incredibly bad taste in shoes. As much as I loved my Grandma Hazel and adored her sister Millie, the women wore ugly, god-awful, hideous shoes. Millie's, which I mentioned before, were best fit for nuns. Cracked, black leather with laces, clunky-heeled, and dowdy, to say the least. From the corner of my eye, as a little girl, I remember snatching glimpses of those creepy things, imagining them to be two fat black birds, perched on aunt Millie's pudgy feet.

Then there were Grandma's. I had never seen anything quite like her style, and thankfully haven't since. To begin, the pair was white, making them somehow more noticeable. Sandal-like, yet frumpy, they were strapped behind the heel with a wide leather band that covered the top of the foot, leaving toes exposed. That band, to make matters worse, was woven into an unusual sort of lattice-like pattern, which did nothing for the shoe, though it did leave the tops of the feet branded with that same crisscrossed pattern for hours after the shoes had been removed.

To top things off, this one-of-a-kind design sat atop a wedge heel that today *might* pass as funky or even fashionable. But back then, believe me, it was not.

Granted, the shoes were well made, sensibly priced and remarkably comfortable, despite that indelible leather band. At least that's what Grandma "Mimi" claimed. But they looked disgusting, especially to a twelve-year-old girl.

What's worse, once Grandma Hazel retired from her job at Troy Laundry, where she stood endless hours over the steamy, hot rollers, coercing stubborn wrinkles out of linen sheets, table clothes, napkins and drapes, she no longer had use for those ridiculous clod hoppers.

So she gave them to my mother!

I could have shriveled up and died the morning my mom appeared at breakfast in her favorite lemon-yellow housecoat and Grandma's hand-me-downs.

"These are heavenly!" she gushed. "I doubt I will ever take them off. They are like walking on marshmallows!"

Speechless, I stared at her feet as my jaw fell open, though little air was being exchanged in my stupor. Surely she was kidding. Somehow a grandmother could get away with such a blatant fashion "don't," but not a mother of an adolescent girl, and definitely not mine.

All too familiar with my mother's strong will and temper, I turned back to my shredded wheat, thanking God that it was not Mom's day to drive car pool. I told myself I'd have to figure out something between now and the next morning, when she would be driving my younger brother, me, Betsy Holler and her sister Marjorie, and that catty Jerrianne Airhart to school.

If I arranged things carefully, the three outsiders would sit in the rear seat. I'd have to check beforehand, but doubted they could see over the front seat down to my mother's feet from their vantage point. Or so I hoped.

That evening as I set the table for dinner I casually asked my mother, who was still wearing the shoes, and still marveling at their comfort, "Do you intend to wear those outside the house?"

"Well, I am certainly not going to wear them to dinner parties or bridge club, but they'll be fine for running around town," she assured me. But I was not to be assured.

And I wondered where Girl Scout meetings, (she was a co-leader) and her volunteer work in our school library might fit in.

Surely, she wouldn't.

To my great relief things went smoothly over the next few weeks, as my mother's busy life seemed to work into an acceptable routine all centered, in my adolescent, self-absorbed mind, on her "new" shoes. I was right about the view, or lack thereof, from the rear seat of the car, and simply had to make it perfectly clear that no one other than family was allowed up front.

The shoes, so far, were a well-kept family secret.

Then one fateful day, I made an oversight, and it was grave. I neglected to consider my mother's role in Saint Paul's Altar Society, a group of pious, dedicated parish women who volunteered on a weekly basis to clean the church sacristy and altar. As I recall, Mom was Vice President and a very active member of the group. And I distinctly remember that Friday was cleaning day at our church.

Coincidentally, Friday was also the day choir practice was conducted for all seventh and eighth graders at Saint Paul's School.

Saint Paul's Catholic Church was built in the late 1930s of red brick and mortar in a pseudo Romanesque style. The large, airy structure boasts an impressive main altar where the sacred tabernacle houses the symbolic body of Christ, with two smaller alcoves flanking each side.

The Blessed Virgin Mary stands serenely in the left alcove and St. Francis gazes down at worshippers from the right. Forty-two rows of mahogany pews cushioned in forest green velvet line the body of the church, with a generous, scarlet carpeted aisle sliced through the center.

The twelve Stations of the Cross, carved in stone, are hung around the walls enclosing the main sanctuary, and in the rear there is a glass-enclosed "crying room" for mothers with babies and small children. Over this back room hangs a sizable choir loft supported by two giant wooden beams, accessible by a narrow, winding flight of stairs reached by way of the rear of the church.

From this loft, looking over the enormous old Baldwin organ, one has a magnificent view of the entire church, all the way down and across to the massive crucifix hanging high over the main altar, where the porcelain body of Jesus painfully stretches to cover most of the wooden cross.

I should point out that Saint Paul's interior was by no means light and bright. Rather, it was dark and a little spooky. Large arched, stained glass windows lined the perimeter of the sanctuary, each depicting such sacred scenes as the Annunciation, Nativity, Last Supper, and Crucifixion. These works of art were beautiful to observe, but they allowed nothing more than a stingy bit of daylight to make its way inside our church.

On this particular morning, kind old Mr. Lucas, the janitor, had been certain to turn on every spotlight to illuminate the altar, so neither a speck of dust nor a strand of a cobweb would go unnoticed by the devout cleaning crew.

I return now to that Friday in the springtime, when I was twelve and in seventh grade.

Here we all are, floating high up in the choir loft, some thirty-five adolescent boys and girls, lined up as ordered, and poised to sing. Taller students in the back rows, shorter ones in front, so each of us has a clear, perfect view. Sister Mary Imelda hits the first keys of "Onward Christian Soldiers"—and then I see her.

It is Mom, and it doesn't matter who else. She is crawling across the main altar, some six feet high off the ground, heading for the tabernacle with a dust cloth in her hand. She is wearing an orange, cotton, sleeveless wrap around-dress, with tiny white dots.

And she is flaunting, or so it seems to me, Grandma's darn shoes.

Tears well up in my eyes and I struggle to remember the lines of our hymn. Everyone is singing along, and everyone, I am sure, is watching my mother, showcased there under the spotlight, now balancing herself on the perilously narrow altar cradling the tabernacle.

Still poised on her knees, she stretches her body like some amateur interpretive dancer, reaching toward the sacred fixture. I clinch my eyes, shake my head as hard as I can, and pray to God I will wake up from the horrible nightmare.

But when I raise my eyes for a peek, nothing has changed except my mother's "center stage" position. Now she's strained on tippy toes in those evil shoes, rubbing her dirty rag with reverence, up and down, back and forth across the holy crucifix . . . the focal point of the church.

To be honest, the rest is a blur. How I made it through that thirty-minute session without falling apart, I will never know. After what seemed like days, Sister Imelda ordered us to line up in alphabetical order for lunch. The agony was over, or so I believed.

I did not look anyone in the eye for fear they'd laugh out loud or ridicule me, my mother, or both of us. I counted the cracks in the sidewalk as we headed down to the lunchroom, in the basement of the church. We plowed through the line until we'd gotten to the K's and Mrs. Reilly checked my name off in the lunch book. As I approached the food counter, I looked up to check the day's menu, and I heard her before I actually saw her.

"Yummy, yummy; everything looks delicious today, doesn't it gals?" she bellowed.

Tears flooded my eyes as it became very clear the Altar Society women were having lunch in our cafeteria. I wanted to die as I watched Mom and her shoes at the head of the line.

Quickly, I discarded any notion of ignoring my mother and pretending I didn't see her. I knew her. She would be annoyed and make an even bigger scene of greeting me. So I boldly approached the woman, confident that I could subtly, skillfully chat her back into the dining room where she and her friends belonged, a safe distance away from the students' lunch hall.

There I would get her seated with her feet and those dreadful shoes under their table. Then, knowing full well how these women gabbed, the seventh grade would be finished eating and back in the classroom before my mother and her shoes even thought about making their grand exit to her blinding red Ford station wagon, parked outside.

I admit it was not an especially clever plan, but it worked. No one said a word to me about the whole excruciating incident. But of course I knew it was on their minds and it was a direct reflection on me.

Every now and then, throughout the endless afternoon, I'd catch a glimpse of kids like super cool David Swenson, with his public school floozy of a girlfriend and snazzy Schwinn bike. Or the snooty Janette Altman, who had pierced ears she hid from the nuns and a fluffy white jacket she'd claim was real rabbit fur. They'd be glaring at me with what I interpreted as scorn, as if it were I who wore the most disgusting footwear in the universe.

It struck me that afternoon as the always impeccably dressed Mrs. Holler drove us home from school, that this had been the worst, most humiliating day of my entire life. I could not wait to bolt from the car and into my house where I'd escape into the secure privacy of my own bedroom, behind closed doors.

I headed first to the kitchen for a quick peanut butter and jelly sandwich or two, as I hadn't been able to stomach a thing at lunch. There I was greeted by good old Mom, and her shoes.

"Hi, Nanner how was your day?" she asked breezily, slapping raw ground beef into misshapen patties, then tossing them onto the fire.

I stood speechless, staring at my mother while thinking to myself, "This woman does not have a clue what I think or feel or am."

Dancing Like Crazy

One of Idaho's state mental hospitals is located on the outskirts of Nampa.

Around the turn of the century, when the town was barely more than a smudge on the map, Nampa was selected as the site to build an institution to house the state's mentally retarded citizens, whom today we'd call intellectually disabled. The name of the facility changed over the years from "Sanitarium for the Feeble Minded and Epileptic" to "Nampa State School" to "Southwest Idaho Treatment Center" as it is known today. I am not sure if Nampans were much affected by the decision to house mentally challenged patients near their home. I don't question why the site was chosen, only what the reaction might have been. In my mind it was no big deal; the place already had its share of people who were questionably stable.

Initially, the facility sat next to an expansive farm staffed by residents, and it was largely self-sufficient. Later on, the farm was sold and converted into two municipal golf courses, side by side for some crazy reason. One might wonder, why two adjacent golf courses? Wouldn't one large, sprawling course make more sense?

It also intrigues me that, early on, higher functioning residents at Nampa State cared for those more severely disabled and not able to care for themselves. In my mind if an individual is capable of caring for himself plus an incapacitated person, he or she ought to be out contributing to society, not locked up in a mental institution.

Nampa State School looked much like the cold, dreary asylums you'd see housing the insane in old movies. Several large, rather nondescript, brown, three or four story brick buildings sat in a sort of semi-circle. These structures were connected by cracking gray cement sidewalks slashing through a center yard of patchy grass and weeds.

As a youngster I ended up spending some time at the state school, not for reasons some might suspect. I occasionally visited with some of its less seriously disturbed residents, caroling with my scout troupe at holiday time or delivering baskets for Easter. Several years in the spring, our dance troupe was bussed out to the state school for a repeat performance of our annual recital. I can still picture our group traipsing across the grounds to the dingy auditorium where we performed. I'd peer from the corner of my eye up at row after row of tightly sealed windows with dim overhead lights straining through the flimsy, yellowing paper shades. I never really wanted to get too good a look at the place. God only knew what was going on inside those walls. And the occasional shrill cry of a crazed inmate reminded me I did not want to know.

For years I studied dance—tap, ballet, and some sort of modern interpretive movement—under Mrs. Alva Thatch. Alva, or "Madame Thatch" to her pupils, was a pencil-thin former ballerina with a pointy nose, thin, paper-white skin, and an orange bouffant. She may or may not have been attractive in her day, I couldn't tell. She lived in a small tract house decorated in a stab at *French Provincial*, and she conducted classes in a square, mirrored room of her musty basement.

Alva tended to run late. Many of my memories of dance lessons find me cramped into sitting position on her cold, cement basement steps, lined up and down with at least a dozen young dancers stooped by overflowing dance bags, impatiently waiting for the class ahead to be dismissed.

We'd perch in the dark stairwell amidst a crescendo of whispers and giggles. Every ten minutes or so, Madame Thatch would pirouette out into the hallway in her stretchy black leotard and tights, reeking of cologne. I was impressed with her short, magenta chiffon wrap-around dance skirt, cinching what appeared to be a waist about the size of my neck.

Her wilted warning played like a broken record.

"Dancers, dancers! Silence, not silliness, will help us reach perfection!" She'd deliver this proclamation with her weak chin gallantly hoisting her sharp nose toward the water-stained ceiling.

Upstairs, while Alva schooled us in the fine art of *plié*, arabesque and shuffle-ball-change, her teenage daughter Patsy was usually sprawled out in front of the television, absorbed in the after school line-up. I always felt like a bother as I rang the front doorbell each week, arriving promptly for class. Patsy, who was painfully overweight and out-of-shape, would be forced to maneuver herself up off the couch, abandoning her bowl of snacks, hobble to the door, some three feet away from her station, and welcome us dancers as we dribbled inside. She tended to open the door only half way, so we'd have to wedge through and around her, as she mumbled "Yeah, go on down. There's a mess of 'em down there already." We dancers seemed like an imposition on Patsy, who appeared to be a troubled young woman. I wished she'd get out of that oppressive house more often, where she was daily faced with imposing hordes of lithe, skinny, wannabe dancers.

Alva's husband, Dick Thatch, was a junk food distributor. I am sure he didn't call himself that, but he drove a big white truck around the county delivering Clover Club Potato Chips, Fritos, Cheetos, Cracker Jacks, Planter's Peanuts, Jiffy Pop—cases of cholesterol, which we didn't know much about back then.

I'd see his distinctive truck buzzing around town, covered in snappy, colorful logos. But I rarely saw Mr. Thatch. His snack food business seemed to require long hours that kept him away from Alva and Patsy much of the time, and they rarely mentioned him.

Madam Thatch was into themed recitals with elaborate, albeit amateur-looking sets, flamboyant costumes and blaring music. One recital that stands out in my mind is "Under the Big Top." At ten years old I was featured in a solo tap number. This was not just any tap dance. Going with the circus theme, I donned a brilliant fire engine red satin jacket with tails. I am sure my mother worked on that costume for weeks, putting the finishing touches on the work of art up to the last minute.

A ruffled white satin shirt burst out from between my lapels, and excruciatingly uncomfortable black, mesh stockings smothered my lanky, adolescent legs. From atop my coifed head rose an elaborate crown of fake, multi-colored feathers, standing at attention.

I was a tap dancing animal trainer in the circus. And the rope in my hand was not only for taming the dancing lions, tigers, and bears, but for skillfully jumping through as I tapped my way across the imaginary circus ring to the popular tune "Elephant Walk."

The trick was to twirl the rope just fast enough that it would not snag on my towering headdress, yet slowly enough that I was able swiftly tap a shuffle-ball-change in between twirls.

I have to admit my number was quite a hit, and I heard a lot of people commenting on my performance after the show.

"That Kilmer girl did a great job! That can't be an easy feat; tapping and taming at the same time."

A few weeks later, our sell-out show was taken on the road to the State school, where we entertained some of the state's less fortunate residents. I have to admit, our follow-up performance brought down the house.

By the time I was a chubby teenager and beyond dancing in public or even at the mental institution, the home had become drastically overcrowded. State authorities decided that not all of the patients housed at the school were clinically insane, and that some could function in society with special guidance. So the authorities announced that a number of the "less disturbed" residents of the Idaho State School would be released into our community. Once released, the state would help these newly freed individuals find employment in service jobs around the town, along with suitable housing.

I must admit, this idea disturbed me. I lost sleep pondering guys like Charlie, the psychotic redhead with acne who loudly slobbered, "Pretty dancers! Pretty dancers!" as he rocked back and forth at the foot of the stage while we performed. The thought of the guy pumping our gas next time we filled up at the station unnerved me.

I felt justified regarding my unrest about this infiltration of some of the state's mentally unstable into the town in which I was living. As a rather innocent girl of fourteen, I was intimidated enough by any male other than my family and maybe Willie Awker, but the thought of encountering an off-balanced member of the opposite sex bagging my groceries or collecting my movie tickets rattled me. For months, I lived in terror.

As it turned out, Charlie the rocker was never released from Nampa State. Rather, borderline patients like Kristy, the learning impaired albino who clumsily helped set up chairs at our recitals; Benny, the tall, learning-disabled, if not talented, center for the home's basketball team; and Sissy, the lazy-eyed woman I'd taught to swim, were set free. These harmless people were placed in appropriate jobs around town, and transported home each evening to supervised living quarters not far from the school.

Kristy became a friendly face at Nampa Bowl, where she dutifully handed out mostly the right sized shoes to eager customers ready to make a strike. Benny kept jumping as an assistant coach for the youth sports program at the community center, and Sissy peddled concessions and shelved swimmer's baskets at the municipal swimming pool.

The situation was not nearly as threatening as I had feared. I decided state officials had been correct in their evaluation of the situation; there were a significant number of residents confined to the hospital who probably should never have been institutionalized. Living in such an environment, they indeed might have become further debilitated. Most of these individuals, whom today we might call "developmentally challenged," did well, even flourished, living amongst the docile residents of Nampa.

The author, age 9, tapping, twirling, twinkling.

As the exodus from Nampa State continued, I was excited by the thought of so many inmates being liberated. Witnessing those prisoners being set free from a trap where they must've felt stifled and out of place inspired me.

One day, I too would escape.

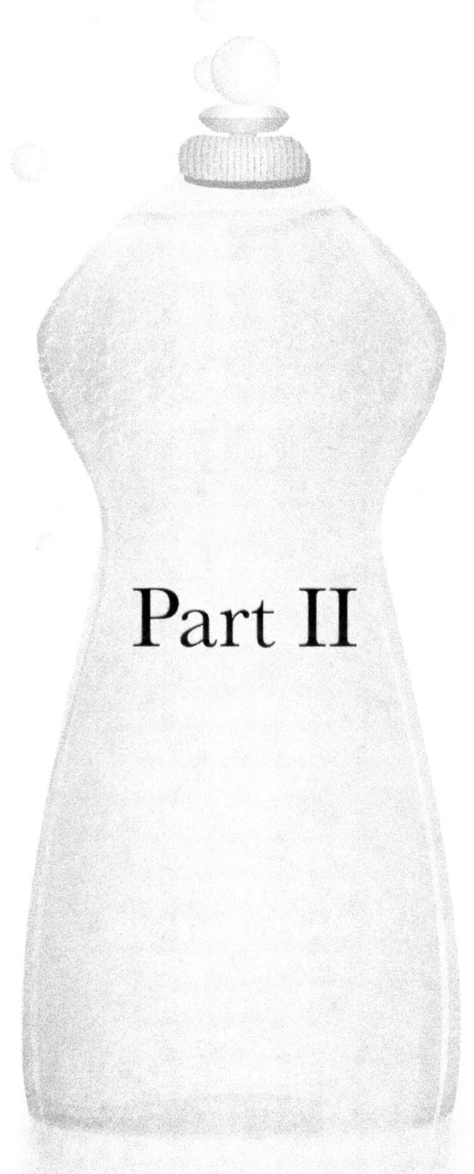

Part II

Class Acts

Nampa behind me, I found myself in Spokane, Washington where I faithfully attended classes at Gonzaga University, a small Jesuit school drawing a diverse student body from around the country.

The roommate assigned to me freshman year was a perfectly nice, seemingly intelligent nuclear science major from Walla Walla, Washington, home of the state penitentiary and sweetest onions on earth. I had heard locals like to brag about their home: "The town so nice they named it twice!"

Chanel might have been acceptable enough had she only taken a shower now and then. Bathing was just not her thing, thus some of us on our floor took to calling the girl "Daisy" behind her back. The odor got so bad after a few months I discussed the stinky situation with our Resident Assistant, a flaky senior from California who spent most of the day in flowery flannel pajamas writing love letters and poems for some phantom guy living in Hawaii. After learning about my ripe roommate, she promised to talk to Daisy in an attempt to urge her into the shower. My sharp sense of smell and keen powers of observation convinced me the wimpy woman never mustered the nerve to discuss personal hygiene with the rank coed in room #213.

Thus I began to make a major production of bathing several times a day, announcing emphatically, "I think I will take another nice, hot, refreshingly invigorating shower, Chanel! Isn't it great the stalls are right around the corner?" She'd nod approvingly then bury her head back in some thick science book. She was a smart girl, but lacking in some basic common sense.

Eventually Daisy snagged a dopey boyfriend from one of the Dakotas who apparently had no sense of smell or simply did not mind body odor. Fortunately, she spent most of her time at this guy's dorm. I'd prop the window open every day as I bolted out to class, and the foul air soon dissipated—somewhat. Sure, the girl's clothes still reeked, but I made sure her closet door was tightly shut, and I hid an open box of baking soda behind her empty laundry basket. I convinced myself my roomie was considerably larger than I, so would never think of trying to borrow anything from my pitiful wardrobe of bell-bottom jeans, T-shirts, sweaters, and the one frumpy dress I owned but seldom wore.

I had managed to escape Nampa with its pungent, permeating stench, yet seemed destined in life to deal with an array of other less than pleasant aromas.

Otherwise, I found university life rather agreed with me and proudly claim to have been one of the few "Zags" I knew who actually attended most of my classes. The structure provided by college seemed to somewhat ease my chronic anxiety. That and the rowdy weekend keggers and late night pig-outs in the dorm helped take the edge off my angst as well. I consistently made the A honor roll, so as a studious sophomore, I decided I'd apply to spend my junior year abroad in Florence, Italy, where Gonzaga has sponsored an extension program since 1963. Little did I know at the time, I was headed toward one of the more life altering adventures of my life, an experience that helped me discover the real me, while forging friendships that have defied time, distance and old age. Never mind the added fifteen—or was it twenty?—pounds and considerable drop in my G.P.A. Eventually I learned to relax and have a good time every now and then.

If the hop from puny Nampa to the booming metropolis of Spokane had proven relatively seamless, that next leap across the Atlantic posed some hurdles. After all, even though my roots were in a Podunk town, I had travelled to exotic locales in my youth; places like Las Vegas, San Francisco, Los Angeles, Washington, D.C., even New York City. But these hot spots were still in good ole America, Mom and Dad were chaperones, dealing was done in dollars, and everyone spoke my language. Well, most everyone.

Having survived a raucous charter flight from Seattle to Amsterdam, nearly one hundred of us jet-lagged, giddy, hung-over American kids took off on a boisterous week-long bus tour through Germany and Austria. We arrived in early September at what was to be our home for the next year. Florence—or *Firenze* as we quickly learned to refer to *our* city—looked even more amazing than all the pictures I had studied in my Italian books back in Spokane.

For nearly forty years, select groups of Gonzaga-in-Florence students attended classes in Antinori Palace, a Renaissance-style stone building in the heart of Florence, occupied by the famous Italian winemakers of the same name. Nampa may have had its version of a palace thanks to Colonel Dewey, but this place, built in the 1400s during the reign of Lorenzo di Medici, was beyond anything I could have fantasized about or seen on television.

Picturing nearly a hundred rowdy young Americans scampering up to classes on the second floor now seems absurd. In our ratty jeans, dingy sweatshirts and scruffy boots, we must have horrified the dignified family residing inside.

We unrefined kids were not allowed into the stately courtyard and lush gardens on the ground floor, nor were we to touch the ancient works of art, majestic statues, and priceless tapestries scattered throughout the building.

I am quite certain the Antinori dynasty breathed a sigh of relief when, in 2003, Gonzaga moved their expanding study abroad program to a larger, more modernized, technologically-friendly facility near the Academia, which houses Michelangelo's famous *David*. I doubt many tears were shed by those refined, influential Florentines.

Classes were held four days a week for us "Gonzagini" as we came to call ourselves, leaving three-day weekends for exploring the city and traveling as extensively as time and our bank accounts would allow. In addition, our package for the year included an action packed, two-week group tour through the Middle East over Christmas break, including such exotic destinations as Turkey, Lebanon, Cyprus, Israel and Greece. Celebrating baby Jesus' birthday in the place he was born was special, albeit tacky with rickety souvenir stands lining the narrow, winding streets of Bethlehem. Pushy vendors madly peddled miniature mangers, plastic holy family figurines, and garish T-shirts flaunting the sacred nativity scene. Upon hearing "Away in a Manger" each holiday season since then, I envision a less heavenly setting for the birth of the little Lord Jesus.

As a psychology major, I ventured to Vienna, Austria in February to complete an independent study on the work of Austrian neurologist/psychiatrist/philosopher Viktor Frankl, a Holocaust survivor who struggled to find some meaning in his captivity. He later wrote a book *Man's Search for Meaning* based on his horrendous experiences in Auschwitz. I studied Frankl's work with genuine interest, eager to relate his profound thoughts and feelings to my otherwise unremarkable existence. If anyone should be anxious and depressed, I surmised, it should be Victor Frankl, for god's sake, not me.

Spring break whizzed by with my beau and a few other classmates as we maneuvered our rented Fiat down the coast of Spain. We frittered away most of the week working on mounds of paella, liters of sangria and our suntans. In May, with classes over and finals behind us, my amour and I gallivanted along the white sand and crystal blue waters of Tuscan beaches, dreading the upcoming day we'd be forced to return to the real world, which we now had trouble referring to as home.

I was not at all surprised to fall in love *with* Florence but did not expect to fall in love *in* Florence. This was not part of my plan. Like Forester's Lucy Honeychurch, I got my room with a view AND a man in this most romantic of cities, if only for a few fleeting months. A free-spirited Californian caught me off guard. Sure, he was handsome and witty, but it was his quirkiness and unpredictability that captivated me. Luigi and I connected while studying together for an Ethics exam; it just seemed like the right thing to do. One thing led to another and before long he was sneaking into my pensione at night and we were planning our last escapades through the Italian countryside. Our final days together in Florence were magical yet agonizing as we faced the dreaded day we'd be forced to part ways and return to the real world. Alas, not long after returning to reality, my first true love would brush me off as quickly as he'd won me over, not for another coed, but for medical school. It seems I was a distraction from his lifelong goal of becoming a physician like his father, or so he tried to console me years later, when we finally spoke again at a reunion.

And so, my wobbly, wonderful world of travel, foreign studies and romance quickly crumbled as my year abroad came to a bitter end. I cried my way from Rome to New York, where my parents waited at Kennedy airport to greet a new and (I wanted to believe) sophisticated, worldly young woman.

Wounded and floundering, I pulled myself together to complete my less than titillating senior year back in what I now considered very unsophisticated Spokane, graduating magna cum laude with not one but three diplomas. Truth be known, having made it to most classes and taken copious notes, I agreed to lend my scribbles to several classmates whose names I will omit here and who slept through most classes. Not total fools, they had also made certain they arrived early for exams and arranged to sit within eye-shot of my desk and the test atop it. More than once I asked myself, "Now who is the smarter person here?"

In appreciation, a couple of my more prudent pals graciously handed over their diplomas to me shortly after our graduation ceremony. Both loveable, lazy oafs commended me with a slap on the back. “You earned this Brainiac! Congratulations!”

Odd Jobs

A major problem with completing college, I quickly realized, is the delusion that one can then easily establish a career. This did not prove to be true for many of us graduating during the economically rocky seventies. Unless you counted slinging bratwurst and pastrami sandwiches and slippery mugs of beer a few nights a week in Spokane's Bavarian Pavilion, I was among the unemployed. And I was yet to face some of life's harder lessons.

Weary of Spokane and sporadic summer waitressing, and disillusioned with being a college grad, I vowed graduate school was in my future. However, I first wanted a job on dry land that did not involve serving food or wearing a bathing suit. So I emptied my skimpy bank account of hard-earned waitressing money, packed up my meager belongings and caught a flight to Washington, D.C., where my older sister lived along with my friend Jas, whom I had met while studying in Italy. Jas was also jobless and was living back home with his parents in Bethesda, a nearby suburb. I, on the other hand, was sleeping on a couch in my sister's friend's basement. Both of us felt like pathetic, down-and-out bums, so we mostly hung out together in commiseration. We spent our days baking popovers and eating the whole batch, driving around in my sister's tiny Austin American sedan we referred to as "The Flintstone Mobile," puffing on cigarettes and slurping cheap wine.

The only gainful, if pitiful, employment we had for months was at the local pharmacy, Bradley Drugs, in downtown Bethesda. Granted, the job was only twice a month for one hour, but it was at six o'clock in the morning, which was usually only a few hours after I had gone to sleep. So this was not exactly a "cushy" job. Myself, Jas, his idle dad who had recently retired from the Atomic Energy Commission, and his tiny, bubbly mother, "Kitten," were official "breathers." We'd show up every other Friday at the crack of dawn, without having brushed our teeth since the previous night. In the backroom of the store we'd share some of our stale breath, blowing through silver- dollar sized holes cut out in a cardboard, makeshift wall. After gargling with various new mouthwashes, we exhaled nine or ten long breaths into the holes, where poor testers on the other side of the wall were forced to smell our hot air and report on the effects, if any, of each oral rinse on our deadly "morning mouths."

For this service we were each paid fifteen dollars for a job that actually took less than a full hour. Afterwards, "Mr. G.," my friend's dad, often took us to breakfast at a local coffee shop, where we joked about our "work" and pondered the possibilities for real jobs for the two of us. Kitten never failed to liven the conversation with her hilarious banter about celebrities and neighborhood gossip, so all in all those were fun mornings despite the early hour.

I bet breakfast for the four of us cost as much or more than Mr. G.'s earnings for the morning, although I am sure he *breathed* more for diversion than dollars.

The *real* job Jas got was picking up sticks and other yard debris for a wealthy family in his neighborhood. He liked the hours, roughly two till five in the afternoon, and could walk to work. I often picked him up at "closing time" in my sister's car, if it happened to start that day. The end of his shift coincided with his parents' evening cocktail hour which worked out nicely for us. More often than not I was invited to stay for dinner, more than a treat for me as I had so little cash in those days.

I considered the next job I scored as barely a step above picking up sticks. I found a position as a night receptionist at Capitol Park Towers, a ten-story apartment building in southwest Washington, D.C. The complex was only four or five blocks from the townhouse where I was existing in the basement.

I was required to be on duty behind the front desk in the center of the huge lobby at 5:00 p.m. Saturday through Thursday, Friday being my one day off. I worked eight hours each night, getting off at one o'clock in the morning. I got no break, which did not matter because after the five o'clock "rush hour" of residents arriving home from work and asking me all kinds of questions and making all sorts of demands, the desk was relatively quiet aside from singles who freshened up and headed out into the bustling city for Happy Hour, dinner, more drinks, dancing, clubbing, whatever. They tended to come home before I was off work during the week, but on weekends who knows when and if they finally got back to their apartments.

During the quiet hours, from about eight or nine until I got off work, I read, wrote, filed my nails, talked on the phone (and pretended it was a "business" call if someone walked by), or chatted with the night security guard. He was a friendly, thirty-ish black guy in an official dark blue uniform, who was shorter and probably weighed less than I. I was carrying extra pounds at the time thanks to all the popovers, wine and lack of exercise. Plus, I slept until noon most days, then caught *The Young and the Restless* in the early afternoon while consuming huge brunches of cheap food like Spaghetti O's, Kraft Mac n' Cheese, or cheap canned tuna that could pass as cat food.

Before I knew it, 4:30 would roll around and it was time to get ready for work. I could wear whatever I wanted, so usually it was my favorite bell-bottom jeans and a presentable top, as this was really all my "customers" saw as I sat behind the desk and greeted them. I did not even have to leave my chair to open the door, as although it was locked around the clock, I had a buzzer that automatically opened the door for those I saw fit to enter *my* building.

"Officer Mike," I respectfully called the security guard, strutted around the complex trying to look tough and I liked to imagine he had a small handgun under his shirt, but realized he probably didn't. Most nights we talked about the more eccentric residents of the building, others he told me about his love life, or lack thereof. He was always courteous and respectful, and I grew fond of him—just as a friend.

One of the more bizarre characters living in Capitol Park Towers was a colorful old woman who introduced herself to me as Doris. She appeared to be in her late sixties or early seventies, although her bleached pink hair and teased up french twist might have been deceiving; maybe she was eighty and had kept a few of her wits about her. She wore the same orange, red and yellow polyester caftan every night, and I never saw her leave the building. She confided in me that she was a retired widow, her husband having passed from unknown causes a few years earlier, and she was a former receptionist for a prominent dentist on Capitol Hill. She worked for the man for almost forty years and had met dozens of renowned politicians.

"Oh, the stories I *can't* tell you!" Doris boasted. "I could write a book if I could find a new ribbon for my old Underwood." Since Doris never left the building and had all her groceries and meds delivered, I was half-tempted to find a stationery supply store and buy her a nice new black typewriter ribbon. Sorry to say, I never get around to that good deed. Besides, I had always had a book to write myself . . .

One particularly dull evening I was reading an old *McCall's* magazine and heard the elevator doors open, presenting Doris in her colorful gown. She was carrying a small, purple, plastic cosmetic case and grinning from ear to ear. I didn't notice her hair was disheveled until she coyly asked me "Nan, dear, can you be so kind as to take these hairpins (unzipping her clutch) and fix these strays back here?"

She pointed to several white, wispy hairs drooping down the back of her neck. Always wanting to please, I proceeded to sweep Doris' hair into a tight, neat bundle, pinning it securely in place. The old woman then pulled a large can of Breck Super Hold from the pocket of her billowing garment, spraying frantically as I covered my eyes and sneezed.

Once I could open my eyes I caught sight of Officer Mike through the glass front doors, who appeared to be laughing out loud.

Every night the slight security officer walked me home—or every morning I should say. I was taller and heavier than he was, like I said, yet I felt no threat whatsoever ambling through the creepy D.C. darkness to the safety and comfort of the townhouse I was calling home.

I worked at Capitol Park Towers nearly six months when I decided night work was not my thing so signed up with Kelly Girls, a chain of temporary employment agencies with offices in the D.C. area. One of the first temp jobs I got was as a receptionist at a local office of the American Cancer Society, in nearby suburban Virginia. A huge poster of a lung infested with sickening cancer hung on the wall across from my desk, and I vowed to myself never again to smoke another cigarette. This job lasted only a few days but the effects of that vivid illustration of a blackened, festering organ will last forever.

It was not long before I was called to type letters at a place called the American Society for Public Administration, better known as ASPA. This gig turned into a semi- permanent deal when my boss, a smelly old white-haired Italian named Manny, realized I could actually write and hired me to be his assistant. Many days I just sat at my desk in a small cubbyhole overlooking Connecticut Avenue, staring out at the meandering pedestrians and traffic. Others I composed dull, monotonous letters to public administrators around the country.

Seriously, in my year and a half I was employed by ASPA, I could not get a firm grasp as to what the organization actually did, so I contented myself with a bi-monthly paycheck in a larger amount than I had ever earned in my sketchy career. I mainly credit the society for instilling in me a strong desire to return to school in pursuit of a degree that might point my life in a more meaningful direction—or at least lead me to a job with a description that made a bit of sense to me.

Watts Next

It was the late seventies when I resigned from my meaningless position with ASPA and flew home to Idaho. There, I packed my crippled old Toyota Corolla with all my earthly possessions and headed for the University of Southern California, where I had been accepted into the school's new master's degree program in gerontology. I had always adored my grandparents, not counting my cold, East Coast grandma, and admired most old people for simply hanging in there. So I figured, with my degree in psychology, the field of aging might be practical. After all, we all get old at some point, god willing, so I presumed I'd always have clients.

The U.S.C. campus, with its Leonard Davis School of Gerontology, is located in Watts, one of L.A.'s more crime-ridden areas. Not one week of grad school had passed before some hoodlum roaming the off-campus parking lots smashed the windshield of my pathetic little car into a million pieces. So negotiating for a new, affordable windshield kicked off my grad studies, and within the week I had purchased a campus parking permit. I lived, learned, and grew poorer with each passing day.

Grad school offered more than its share of anxious moments, from dreading exams to being swallowed up by a giant earthquake or perhaps driven into oblivion off the bulging L.A. freeways. Suffice it to say I endured the two-year program, earned a master's degree in Gerontology, and realized this was a field that could drive me further into the depths of anxiety and depression.

Initially I had convinced myself that working for the good of the elderly would be immensely rewarding. That was until I was assigned a field placement in a rather dark, dingy retirement home just north of Long Beach. Each week I took part in a discussion group consisting of six senior residents, a therapist and myself.

After the first few sessions of quivering and fighting back tears, I realized I might not be cut out for the field of gerontology.

Mr. A., an artist, was going blind and could no longer paint, much less read, or take long walks. Mrs. B. had suffered a debilitating series of strokes, thus her lifelong love of ballet was left to her imagination. And Mr. C., suffering from diabetes, Parkinson's and so many ailments, could only mutter, "My body is driving me out of my mind."

I began losing sleep at night fretting about these hopeless old folks and decided it was in my best interest to pursue a career doing something more uplifting. I convinced myself the past two years and thousands of dollars had not been spent in vain. After all, I had studied gerontology from every angle, so figured all I had learned might serve me well should I live to an old age.

So I re-packed the less than trusty Toyota, picked up my diploma, half-heartedly bid farewell to the city of Angels and headed east on Route 66, determined to return to D.C. and start some sort of respectable life with a job, friends and a decent place to live. Studying the map, I estimated the trip would take approximately six days if my car cooperated, and I'd spend my nights in cheap hotels, usually near truck stops just off the interstate. I was sure to shove a large dresser or heavy chair in front of the bolted, chained door while I slept, intending to call the burly man at the front desk should I detect an intruder. I found this reassuring until I realized the culprit might well be that guy at the front desk—with a key to my room.

No one bothered me much during my cross-country trip, unless you count the obnoxious truck drivers blasting their horns, threatening to force me off the road, passing me with creepy smiles, then, once out ahead, slowing down, just for kicks.

I did run into some nice enough guys one night while lost in a deluge outside Knoxville, Tennessee. With darkness looming in torrential rain, I noticed lights from a large dwelling off in the woods several hundred feet from the country road. Pulling into the long driveway I could see into a well-lit area, apparently a dining room, with about a dozen people seated around a large table. Bolting from my car to the front door, I rang the bell and waited for a response.

Suddenly the large wooden door swung open, revealing a tall man in suspenders and some sort of overalls motioning me inside. "Come on in, little lady," he drawled. "We're just sittin' down for some grub. Come meet the guys!"

Entering the dining room, I stared at the group of men, but not as hard as they stared back at me. In my dripping hair, wet T-shirt, short shorts and bare feet, I squirmed. Spotting the fire pole in the next room I realized I had interrupted dinner at a local firehouse. The way the brawny diners gaped at me, I felt like a mirage.

"What can we get you to eat, darlin'? Spaghetti, meatballs, salad, garlic bread, you name it. You gotta be hungry this time-a-night."

Famished, I ordered the works and wolfed down the heartiest meal I'd had in months.

Then Buck, who'd met me at the door earlier, addressed me.

"Now, we have a spare room in the back and you're welcome to stay, Miss Nan. No one will bother you and you can get a good night's sleep before hittin' the road come mornin'."

"I really appreciate your offer, Buck. But I best get in a few more miles before I hit the hay."

Honestly, I had briefly considered his tempting invitation but decided it wise to move along, lest I tempt some of these manly firefighters.

Driving along the dark, damp highway later that night I decided I had definitely made the right decision, keeping my eye out for a big, bright, blinking "MOTEL" sign offering little more than a place to shut my eyes for a few hours. Uninterrupted, I could only hope.

Six days after leaving sunny California, I pulled into our nation's capital on schedule, my entire body buzzing from driving nearly five hundred miles per day on a sagging bucket seat, shoddy shocks and gallons of Tab cola.

But in some strange sense, I felt I had made it.

Wild Life

I arrived in Washington knowing one thing for sure. I was finished with my formal education; no more school for me. Having considered a career in medicine while studying physiology in California, I quickly dropped the notion when I realized I'd be nearly thirty years old before I could fulfill the grueling requirements to become a physician. And the thought of being over-the-hill and deeply in debt at that point left me cold. I wanted gainful employment, no homework, and a wardrobe of more than grubby jeans and faded T-shirts. It was time for me to become a grown-up career woman.

Crashing with my sister in her Capitol Hill English basement, I began searching the Post's employment pages. I found myself questioning what a psychology/Italian studies major with a master's degree in gerontology might do for a living. The possibilities seemed limited yet I continued to firmly object to serving food or working anywhere near a swimming pool.

A few days into my search, an adorable panda logo caught my eye under a publicity assistant advertisement for a job with the World Wildlife Fund. As fate would have it, my sister was friendly with the Executive Director of the non-profit group, and I quickly scored an interview. For days prior to my meeting I studied up on issues like sea pollution, devastation of tropical forests, endangered animals, declining primate populations and the preservation of plant species worldwide.

I snagged the job without as much as a second interview. The organization needed decent writers if not certified gerontologists, so I was qualified for the position, nebulous as it seemed. I was informed I should float around the office overseeing the contributions department staff, assisting with publication writing, gathering relevant information for the public relations department and helping to orchestrate fundraisers across the country. These events might be luncheons or dinners with influential Washington politicians, socialites, and philanthropists; museum events showcasing WWF's crucial conservation projects worldwide; or lectures and seminars introducing prominent conservationists addressing pressing global concerns.

I loved the job, the cause, my boss, co-workers, and especially the steady paycheck.

One stellar event that stands out in my mind took place at the Smithsonian's then newly opened Hirschhorn Museum of Art. The keynote speaker for the evening was "Sir Sydney Somebody" whose name escapes me not only because of the passing years. I would not want to humiliate the nobleman should he still be alive.

Sir Sydney was to address the illustrious crowd on the imminent danger of the dwindling orangutan population. The species was diminishing throughout the world's tropical forests, and action had to be taken immediately to save these precious apes. Sir Sydney's speech was crucial, and would have been considered poignant had it not been for one fundamental mistake. Throughout the first five or six minutes of his presentation, Sydney pronounced Orangutan as "orange-you-tan." This was not good. Most of the audience squirmed with each mispronunciation, until someone passed me a note folded into a small square of pink paper. I cautiously opened the message, which read, "*N. Please discreetly sneak up onto the stage behind Sir S., and pass him a note to get him to talk about Oh-rang-ga-tans!!!!!! This is absurd!*"

Great. I had been selected to do the dirty work. I obliged, successfully delivering the note to the speaker: "It is Oh-rang-ga-tans, Sir," I carefully instructed him. He then as smoothly as possible apologized and continued his talk about the endangered species. The damage might have been done, but he seemed to feel he had saved face, even if the rest of us were left wondering.

I suppose I so vividly remember that night, as I am a lifelong, devoted fan of monkeys, chimps and apes. I am aware of this passion since my mother often pointed out my early childhood TV-watching habits. She claims I would refuse to watch anything on television unless it featured a primate. You can imagine how this limited my television viewing as a kid.

A highlight of the sixties for me was the Friday evening broadcast of *The Hathaways* which featured Peggy Cass as the mom Elinore, Jack Cassidy as Walter the real estate selling dad, and three lovable chimps they raised as their children. While their friends and neighbors were mildly appalled, I was enthralled by the zany sitcom.

The World Wildlife Fund eventually promoted me to be Assistant to the Director of their corporate office on Park Avenue in New York City, funded at the time by the Philip Morris Corporation. So in addition to a slightly less meager paycheck, more responsibility, and the chance to meet more fabulous celebrities in the Big Apple, every Friday the corporation awarded me a carton of cigarettes. This freebie might have been a bigger bonus had I been a smoker and not a staff member presumably working to help save the environment.

Running with Jackie

It is 1980 and Jacqueline Onassis and I are living in Manhattan. She owns a luxurious Upper East Side penthouse on Fifth Avenue. I rent a closet-of-a-studio directly across Central Park, the sprawling oasis we share as lawn.

Though our views surely differ, I can only imagine hers. A magnificent twelfth-story panorama boasts a vast expanse of lush, billowing treetops, the tip of the Met's glass pyramid whisking sparkles up her way. Joggers below, a string of colorful dots, circle the reservoir. In the distance, towers, turrets, and rooftop gardens etch the skyline.

Hers must be a staggering vista.

My Westside, third-floor, $395 a-month view is real. From the dingy cracked tile of the one-person-at-a-time bathroom, if I crank open the window, balance myself on the radiator, and strain my neck to the right, I can see the park—a speck of it. There's the lower half of several husky tree trunks and during the spring and summer, a smack of promising green. I have a perfect view all year long of the back of the traffic light that disciplines motorists careening through the park on 81st Street, demanding that they *screech* to a halt at Central Park West.

Mine is a noisier view.

Never mind that there are thirteen million people living with me and Jackie in New York City. I feel somehow connected to her. I have come here to start a life for myself; she to reinvent hers. We are both New Yorkers, though she precedes me by more than a decade. Plus, people say we look alike.

For months it has been happening, since I arrived in the city—people commenting on my resemblance to the young Jackie. More than one chatty cab driver has babbled away to his rearview mirror about how he's driven her here or there, telling me,

"Ya know, little lady, you're a dead ringer for Jackie Kennedy. Anybody ever tell ya that? You're prettier though, I swear."

"Oh, thanks" I mutter, rather annoyed at being compared to someone that old.

A velvety-skinned beauty consultant at Bergdorf Goodman's, gushes. "Darling, you are the young Jackie O! Everyone has a twin somewhere in the world, and we've found Jackie's!"

Construction workers heckle me. "Hey Jackie! Woo hoo!"

Andro, my Serbian doorman, goads me for an autograph and my friends begin to teasingly call me Jackie.

There are some eleven thousand homeless people in the city of New York at any given time. One of them spends his days haunting the street in front of D'Agostino's, the food market just around the corner from by apartment building. He is a derelict my friends and I jokingly refer to as "Derel" as we don't know his real name.

If at first you don't see him, you smell him.

When not sitting in a stupor, Derel darts about the street like a life-sized, wind-up toy, draped in his raincoat that looks like it might have been used to scrub down a subway station. Ratty, black, lace-less high-top sneakers gnaw at his scrawny ankles, crusted with grime and caked blood. Derel has more hair than Janis Joplin, a mane that has been neglected into matted, gnarled, greasy ropes of twine that seem to be strangling his wobbly little head with its slippery stone eyes.

The poor bum's teeth are either black with rot or gone; darkness lurks between those parched, nicotine-stained lips. Derel flaunts what appears to be his magic wand, a partially scorched white plastic spatula that seems important to him.

Waving this sacred prop in front of his face like some high priest at benediction, Derel might exclaim,

"Jesus hates cops!"

"Don't give yer babies drugs!"

Or,

"You're hurtin' me man!"

It depends on who he believes he is at that moment in time.

Derel's personalities vary, but never his request. "Gotta quarter for a cup-a-coffee?" he cackles to most anyone who passes by, not so much out of any real need, just curiosity or the desire to connect. Maybe he is coherent enough to realize a coffee for twenty-five cents is unheard of in this city.

Only a fool believes it is coffee the bum craves.

Every five or six months, Derel disappears for a few days, to return looking like a new man, if only by outward appearances. Authorities haul him in for a de-lousing of sorts. He's back on the street in no time, cleaned up, and missing five or six inches of hair—what's left of it curls after shampoo. His overcoat is as spotless as it will ever be again, and they've spared him his spatula.

So we are sure it's really our Derel.

I am beginning to feel like I know this delusional neighbor, though I never really acknowledge his presence. Sensing him, I discreetly cover my nose and proceed on my way to shop or work or take in a little more of the big city.

It is the same routine each time I pass.

"Jackie! Hi! Gotta quarter for a cup-a-coffee?"

Derel calls me Jackie too, and I suspect my good friend Susie Case has tipped him off as to my nickname, so I play along for fun. I convince myself the man was sober and sane during the Camelot era, and toys with hazy memories of the dead president's dreamy wife.

Since these days Derel's mind is not grounded in reality, it occurs to me that he might believe I am the former first lady. Sometimes I wonder if at night, perched on a steamy grate on some dark side street, he brags to his homeless cronies over a bottle of Thunderbird or Boone's Farm.

"Saw Jackie Kennedy again today; ya know, she lives on my block."

And they believe him.

It is Halloween night of that same year, and perhaps I have crossed the line. I blame it on Susie, who is skilled at sewing and persuasion. It is her idea I go to our friend John Corbett's annual costume party as Jackie Kennedy. She makes me do it.

We spend days scouring the resale shops on the upper Eastside, searching for just the right pink suit. We finally spot it at New to You, on Lexington Avenue. For fourteen dollars we come home with a pink satin suit, which according to the label, is from Saks Fifth Avenue.

"This is so cool. I bet it was expensive as heck!" Susie marvels as she sets to work on a navy cotton collar and lapels. We are working from the November, 1963 issue of *Life* magazine we've borrowed from The New York Public Library. It is preserved in a plastic sleeve, and Jackie is on the cover shaking hands with an adoring fan, while cradling those haunting red roses.

Susie's enthusiasm is contagious and I eagerly help her construct a perfect pillbox hat from cardboard and extra pink fabric she has salvaged from the hem, collar and lapels of the Saks suit. The giddy seamstress gloats.

"You will be the perfect Jackie, Nanette!" Another name she likes to call me after a night we met some Frenchmen in Greenwich Village.

The evening of the big party, I borrow my banker roommate's size nine and a half black pumps and stuff the toes with Kleenex to accommodate my size seven feet. Of course, I am aware Mrs. Kennedy's are long. I wear the boat-like shoes with the pink suit, matching pillbox hat, large, ovalish dark glasses, a string of pearls, and white gloves. I carry a dozen plastic red roses, unable to afford the real thing.

Down the street, Susie becomes Wonder Woman. She and the Flying Nun pick me up at my place around nine and we head out to catch a train uptown to Corbett's place, not far from Columbia University. The thought crosses my mind that we'd never see the real Jackie in this neighborhood, but I am not so sure about Caroline or John-John, and am mortified at the prospect.

The party is a smash, and I take home first prize for costume—a bottle of finer wine than most of us can afford. I have always treasured a picture taken of me that memorable night, shaking hands with Wonder Woman.

Years later I will notice that the pink in my, or Jackie's, suit has faded in that old photograph, while "Lynda Carter's" red tube top is vivid as ever. It will seem oddly supernatural.

After the party has dwindled to a few die-hard guests, Susie and I, exhausted, splurge on a taxi home. It's an unusually warm and balmy October night as we clumsily plop out of the cab in front of my apartment building, where we are greeted by Derel and his spatula.

"Good evening, ladies,," he schmoozes. "Gotta quarter for a cup–a-coffee?"

Not a word about my award-winning Jackie costume nor the fact I am with Wonder Woman.

Some weeks after that Halloween party, before the Christmas holidays take over, I spot Jackie Onassis jogging around the reservoir in Central Park. She has tried to disguise herself to look like "one of us." She wears a long black turtleneck sweater and sweat pants, a gray stocking cap pulled low to cover her famous brunette bob. Those trademark oversized dark glasses are pushed up on her head, revealing her telltale, wide-set brown eyes. I instantly recognize something about her, that *whatever it is* that makes her not one of us. At not much taller than my five feet four inches, she floats above everyone. Rather than clomping along the trail like the other panting runners, Jackie glides, never breaking a sweat.

I hit the path running in the opposite direction around the loop. As I nervously pass her the first time, she is squinting in the sunlight, so I focus on her teeth, which are slightly discolored and crooked.

Suddenly I am a little light headed, yet enervated. I pick up my pace, my heart beating stronger, my lungs pumping rhythmically, my legs at full stride.

Next time around I vow I will meet Jackie eye to eye, and smile.

Jackie Kennedy greeting Wonder Woman. Halloween, NYC, circa 1980.

Dating Rituals

Like Jackie, I went to Texas to stand by my man. Fortunately, there I encountered better luck than she, and ended up marrying rather than burying my catch. I had moved to the Lone Star state in pursuit of a husband, not just anyone, but an alluringly low-key New Yorker who'd been transferred to Houston by his employer, an oil company. I'd met him at that Halloween party in Manhattan, dressed as Jackie. He came as an Arab draped in some sort of middle-eastern robe, a flowing white scarf tied around his head with a cord. Blonde, blue-eyed and fair-skinned, he won no prizes that night, unless you counted me.

Introducing himself as Preston, he revealed he had just returned from Iran where he'd spent several years teaching English. Overhearing that he spoke four or five languages and had travelled the world, I straightened my pillbox hat and paid closer attention.

Not long after meeting the bogus Arab I did some snooping and acquired his phone number. Knowing he was working on a business degree at Columbia University, I decided I might need to borrow his library card. This was not a total hoax.

For my job at World Wildlife Fund I actually did need to do some research on mating rituals of orangutans or panda bears or maybe sea turtles—something endangered anyway. Or so I wanted him to believe.

My scheme worked and a few days later we arranged to meet deep in the stacks of Columbia's massive Butler Library. There I managed to acquire not only his card but a little more insight into this enigmatic character who spoke when spoken to and seemed pressed to offer much more than his last name. Next we set a date to meet later in the week at a nearby bistro where I could return his card—and he could impress me with his French, as it turned out.

In retrospect, I suppose I fell in love months later in a World Trade Center elevator. My well-travelled beau kept his money in a bank high up on the 40-somethingth floor of one of the soaring towers. One spring afternoon, I accompanied him to the Trade Center to make a deposit or withdrawal or some such transaction, before sharing sandwiches on a park bench. His business completed, we entered the elevator and as it descended the lift stopped, the doors opening onto a lower floor. Three Middle Eastern-looking men joined us, and Preston addressed them saying something entirely foreign to me, with a conversation ensuing in a language I did not recognize.

As the elevator halted on the mezzanine level, we all scurried off and the mysterious men bid us farewell, first in English and then that other, incomprehensible tongue.

"Um, what language were you speaking with those guys?" I asked, trying to sound casually interested rather than completely flabbergasted.

"Oh, that was Farsi; they are Iranian."

"Why didn't you tell me you speak Farsi?"

He shrugged. "You never asked. It's a pretty easy language to pick up."

By now totally smitten, I wondered what he saw in me, a hick from Idaho.

Maybe he liked potatoes?

Actually, I think I might have won him over revealing one of my few claims to fame. I recall sharing with him that I did not want to brag, but that my cousin Corrie's grandfather, that would be my father's sister's father-in-law, invented the tater tot. The man, Henry Chase, along with the Grigg Brothers, came up with the brilliant idea of clumping potato scraps into little turds, freezing them, selling them to Ore-Ida, and making a small fortune. With this extra cash Henry bought hundreds, maybe thousands of acres of land in central Idaho around Lake Cascade, where we Kilmers now own a rickety yet cozy cabin. Cousin Corrie and her family, on the other hand, enjoy a stunning, lodge-like summer home just down the road from ours.

Never mind. I got the better husband, if you ask me. Not that my cousin's spouse isn't a great guy!

Years later Preston quipped to my father that he'd read Idaho had more millionaires per capita than any state in the nation, which captured his interest more than my looks, personality or chocolate cheesecake. I figure it must have been true love or he'd have dumped me the minute he met my humble dad and discovered he was probably not one of those tremendously wealthy cattlemen bolstering our state's financial status.

And so it happened, nearly five years after that fateful Halloween party, we eloped to my favorite city in the world, succumbing to marriage in Florence. I couldn't help but speak the language having studied in Italy as a college coed, but to my chagrin, my new husband was almost as fluent by the close of our honeymoon. Much to my delight, I realized I had married a polyglot.

Back home, from our condo in Houston, we newlyweds could look out over the monstrous Astrodome, the "Eighth Wonder of the World" according to some proud Texans. Lying in bed late at night gazing out my window, it reminded me of a massive space ship, one I liked to imagine could carry me off to some far away, exotic locale.

Little did I know how quickly my dream would become reality.

Asian Accents

From twelve stories above, I watch the carnival scene below me. Miniature trucks and bumper-like cars whiz up, down and across the narrow streets. Hordes of tiny people are a blizzard of colorful confetti, while toy bicycles weave in and out, up and down, through the maze that is Tokyo.

It was 1985 and we newlyweds were relocating to Tokyo, having endured many long months in the murky shadows of the Astrodome. Once again, I had escaped.

Our home for the next several months, until we found a suitable rental, was the world-renowned Hotel Okura, offering grand, luxurious accommodations in the heart of downtown Tokyo. Truly, we had come a long way from our humble Texas condo. As Preston headed off to work each morning, I was free to wander, and to wonder what I was going to do with myself for the next few years. His assignment was open-ended, so we could only guess how long we would be living in Japan.

Before leaving the U.S., I had begun researching on my own. I quickly learned about a common condition experienced by nearly all newcomers to a foreign land. I was told to expect:

CULTURE SHOCK. This term describes the anxiety and feelings (of surprise, disorientation, confusion, etc.) felt when people have to operate within an entirely different cultural or social environment, such as a foreign country. It grows out of the difficulties in assimilating the new culture, causing difficulty in knowing what is appropriate and what is not. This is often combined with strong disgust (moral or aesthetic) about certain aspects of the new or different culture.

According to experts, the condition manifests itself with a variety of symptoms:

—high phone bills

—depression

—sudden aggressive hostility

—claustrophobia

—nail biting

—rare cancer

—thrombosis

—cravings

—crying spells

—driving accidents

—fear of going outside

—withdrawal from TV.

I decided to disregard the last symptom, given there were few television programs in English in Tokyo at the time.

Around the time we were moving, an article in the *Wall Street Journal* reported China as the most popular destination for Western expatriates, ranking the country second only to Japan for the most failed assignments by expats. The simple reason given: "Families just don't adjust that well."

My new husband and I tried to assure ourselves. Despite such dire warnings, we knew we were adaptable and adventuresome. We knew to expect some rocky moments but with patience and tenacity, we would sail through like troupers.

Young and invincible, we asked ourselves,*What is the worst that could happen?*

An all-expense paid week in Hawaii was an added perk. In route to Tokyo we stopped in Honolulu to partake in an "Introduction to Japan" seminar for a few hours a day, presented by an older American couple who had lived in the country for several years. Never mind that nearly thirty years had passed since that time, and that much of the cultural information presented to us was out of date. We could not complain nor deny that our week in paradise was a boondoggle.

Admittedly, Tokyo intimidated me. I had hitchhiked through Europe, explored the Middle East and vacationed in Mexico, but this place was different. There were few if any signs in English, and my Japanese thus far consisted of "hello," " goodbye," "thank you," and "where is the restroom?" I didn't know a soul other than my new husband and the timid little Japanese maid who tidied our room each morning.

What was worse, my dread of the ground opening up beneath me had resurfaced, so to speak. Many years had passed since my graduate school days in shaky Southern California, but Japan might have been an even greater threat since I could not understand the warnings on the TV and radio. Any public safety alerts, precautions and stabs at quake prediction were beyond me.

There is no denying, Japan is one of the more earthquake-prone countries in the world, perched atop numerous tectonic plates that rub against and agitate each other. This constant friction causes roughly one thousand tremors across the island each year.

One thousand? That is roughly 2.74 rattlings a day! And every time one strikes, it is a reminder that the country's capital, Tokyo, and my new home, is long overdue for the "Big One."

Tokyo's last major quake was in 1923. Seismologists, those clairvoyants who predict these disasters, say another similar eruption should occur every seventy years or so.

This gave me some comfort, as this would mean the next one should not strike until around the year 2003, giving me almost twenty years leeway. Surely, I surmised, we would have left the country by then.

Most of my first weeks in Tokyo I tried to put earthquakes out of my mind as I watched the only English television channel, CNN Headline News. The satellite station also ran a program called "Style," which CNN repeated off and on throughout the day as a break from their monotonous news stories.

Elsa Clench, a tall, thin Australian woman with a shiny black bob, paper white skin and pointed features hosted the program, which featured fashions from around the world. Lanky, starved, exotic models swished across the screen as Elsa described the latest haute couture in her velvety voice.

I rarely observed any apparel a normal woman would consider clothing.

A highlight of my day was greeting my husband in the evenings and deciding on dinner plans. He entertained me with stories from the outside world, mostly about his office in Akasaka, a section of downtown Tokyo not far from our hotel, known for its office buildings, restaurants and sushi bars by day, and neon-lit circus of hostess bars, pubs, and gentlemen's clubs by night.

On several occasions in the early evening, we caught the rare sight of a little man tugging a wooden rickshaw down a narrow back alleyway. He would be transporting a lavishly-garbed Geisha woman to her evening's work.

The more time I spent in Tokyo the more I became fascinated with the Geisha profession. Incorrectly regarded as prostitutes by many westerners, they are generally highly refined, talented performers and musicians. The women are well versed in Japanese aesthetics and are paid generously by patronizing businessmen. During my stay in the country, I later became friends with a creative director, a colleague at the advertising agency where I worked who claimed to be the illegitimate son of a Geisha. Having grown up in a Geisha House in Tokyo, he regaled me with some fascinating stories, tales he preferred I not share with anyone.

Back at the Hotel Okura, non-stop news, Elsa's frivolous fashions and room service quickly grew old, so after nearly a week

I decided it was time to venture out on my own. I planned to take enough yen to catch a cab should I get lost, and asked the concierge in the lobby to write directions back to the hotel in Japanese. I was a little more comfortable by then with the neighborhoods immediately surrounding our hotel, having explored after dinner most evenings.

I had spent years maneuvering the streets of New York City, but nothing I'd experienced compared to Tokyo. This massive city was as crowded every day as Times Square on New Year's Eve. And in addition to the traffic, bicyclists zoomed about everywhere, continuously ringing little bells warning pedestrians to get out of the way, even though there was really nowhere to move.

As we passed the weeks living luxuriously in the Okura, we searched for suitable housing while waiting for our shipment of worldly possessions to arrive from the states. My husband's company was helping us with our house hunting and had provided a consultant named Nakamura who acted as intermediary between us and our real estate agent, Mr. Yamaguchi. An honest, pleasant enough man, he was only willing to show housing that was, in his broken English a *stone's throw* from my husband's office building.

I soon figured out this man did not have a clue what his favorite expression meant, as he showed us living quarters as far away as an hour from Preston's office. We toured dozens of unacceptable apartments in one *mansion* after another. We learned that Japanese refer to most any apartment building with more than two or three levels as a *mansion*. As decadent as hotel living at the Okura might be, we were more than ready to find a home we could call our own.

Otherwise my life was falling into place once I discovered the Tokyo American Club, an oasis of fellow countrymen which truly was a *stone's throw* from our hotel. There did not seem to be many women in corporate jobs in Japan in those days, and I found many expat wives hung out in this club. They lingered over lunch, drank, played mahjong, drank, sun-bathed by the pool, and drank. This was their life and I refused to accept it as mine.

Regardless, I felt comfortable eating a tuna sandwich or burger in the dining room while eavesdropping on people who spoke my language. Weather permitting, I swam laps in the Olympic sized outdoor pool, then from a lounge chair poolside I read or wrote letters to friends and family back in the states.

One day not long after I had discovered the club, I overheard a woman dressed in a business suit talking over lunch about a headhunting agency in Tokyo, specifically catering to western women seeking employment. I perked right up, rushed back to our hotel, and phoned the director of this agency, an American woman whose name I'd been given during lunch.

In a matter of days I had landed a job writing advertising copy for J. Walter Thompson, the fourth largest ad agency in the world, based in New York City. Gaining a work permit in Japan required a ton of paperwork, including proof the job I would be performing could not be carried out by a Japanese, which was not difficult as I would be writing English copy for western consumers.

Also, they informed me I would be required to show proof that my husband, employed by a Japanese subsidiary of a U.S. company, would guarantee my airfare home, should I for whatever reason be evicted from the country. Preston agreed to sign, making me promise I would not commit any crimes in Japan—or at least not get caught doing so.

So I had a job, but still no home. To date, we had looked at over fifty sterile, uninspiring, western-style high-rise condos in the typical gaigin, or expat areas of Tokyo. At the risk of offending Nakamura-san, we finally took matters into our own hands and stumbled upon a charming Japanese/Western style house in the Japanese neighborhood of Sendagi. This residential area was but a ten minute subway ride from downtown Tokyo, thus underground commuting would be a convenient means of transportation for us.

Our Asian dream house was owned by a Japanese physician who seemed apprehensive about renting to foreigners. Nakamura rallied and was able to convince the woman we would be responsible tenants, so before long we had an enchanting new home.

Enormous by Japanese standards, the house was average-sized by ours, especially considering we had been living in Texas. Constructed of white stucco and bright blue ceramic tile roofing, the home was surrounded by a six-foot high mortar wall with a wrought iron entry gate. Once inside the gate, guests passed through a quaint Japanese garden accented by a koi pond with a soothing waterfall. I was interested to learn that the typical Japanese garden is artfully designed to ensure a different plant blooms each month throughout the year.

Inside, the scent of birch wood floors, walls and ceilings permeated the home. A few steps up from the western style, carpeted living room an elevated tatami mat dining room with traditional wood framed, rice paper sliding doors reminded us we were in Japan. The kitchen was equipped with appliances half the size we were accustomed to, adjacent to a small, western style dining area, should we not be in the mood for dining on the floor.

The bath is arguably the most important room in any Japanese home. Ours was basically one large, white, tiled room with a sunken tub, shower and sink. There were no curtains, dividers or screens like back home. The toilet was in a separate, small, unheated closet down the hallway. Come winter, a heated seat was a welcome treat. We often heard unsuspecting guests squeal with delight upon sitting down on our cozy commode.

Upstairs there were three small bedrooms and a study. Some nights we slept in our queen sized bed in the carpeted, western style room, just like home. Feeling more adventuresome, we might choose a tatami room where we'd sleep on the straw matted floor in traditional velvet and silk wedding futons we couldn't resist buying at a local department store.

Once settled in our new home we were amused when Japanese guests came to visit and inevitably inquired, "This house is SO big! Who lives upstairs?"

Apparently, the Japanese found it impossible to imagine two people would live in such an enormous house. Typically living in one, possibly two-room apartments or tiny houses, the natives marveled at what they called our palace.

Wandering through the narrow, cobblestone alleyways winding throughout our neighborhood, I felt as though I were visiting "Little Tokyo" in Disneyworld. Each evening, short, slant-eyed little men in customary navy and white cotton *yukatas*, or robes, clomped along in raised wooden thong sandals, towel over one arm, chatting away as they headed for their communal bath. Some stared at me with my big round eyes and tall stature. At nearly five feet four inches I relished feeling statuesque in this exotic new world.

There was no denying we were the new *gaigin* neighbors and the talk of the town. No one spoke to me but I felt their eyes on me. I might have been the first foreigner some of them had seen in person. I braced myself as I walked through our neighborhood; to be inconspicuous seemed impossible. Caught staring, neighbors would quickly look away at the sight of me hobbling home from the subway stop loaded down with bags of groceries. In the local supermarket, shoppers were curious about what I might be purchasing, peeking into my basket. Little did they know I might be buying sushi-grade tuna to grill for our dinner; cooking such a delicacy would surely be considered a crime.

We wondered if we were welcome in the neighborhood or not; it was difficult to tell. Then one night not long after we had moved in, an older man rang the bell outside our front gate. Shocked to have a caller, and unable to see who it was from the house, Preston walked through the garden to open the gate.

A little man he recognized as our next door neighbor, swinging a bamboo-handled broom back and forth, was babbling nervously in Japanese as he demonstrated how to sweep the street.

Mortified, we got the message that in Japan, each resident is responsible for keeping the narrow street in front of his house clean. From then on, we dutifully swept the alleyway in front of our house each morning before heading to work. And we wondered what other rules we were breaking as we tried to fit in as upstanding citizens of Sendagi.

Other than perhaps the Germans, I had never seen people so obsessed with cleanliness. Workers in pristine uniforms scrubbed the subway floors and walls each morning. Women in white gloves polished handrails, doorknobs and light posts. Men were constantly scouring the streets by hand with buckets and brushes. There was no rest for window washers. Once every window from the ground up to the top floor of a building had been washed, workers immediately returned to start washing again on the ground floor. Laborers were distinguished by their unique, stylish, costume-like uniforms, which seemed to add dignity to even the most menial of tasks.

Despite the fact that the Tokyo metropolitan area boasted one of the most sophisticated underground transit systems in the world, the ride was not always pleasant. Commuting on the immaculate, efficient, punctual subway train to work each morning had its ups and downs.

Underground, these seemingly polite, sensitive individuals could instantly transform themselves into heathens. Stern little men wielding small wooden clubs did not hesitate to whack stragglers on the back, should they not be shoving hard enough to squeeze into a car already overflowing with harried commuters.

There were times I had to fight for each breath of air, so tightly was I packed into a train car. What was worse, it was not uncommon for otherwise proper gentlemen to fondle any woman squished up against him; no body part seemed off-limits. A nosy passenger might read my letter from home over my shoulder. And mischievous school children seemed to be having fun stomping on the toes of my favorite designer pumps.

One on one, I decided, most of these people were gracious and genteel. Throw them into a crowd, and they can become rude, almost barbaric. I had heard some refer to this as the Japanese herd mentality. Not that most of us Americans are so refined . . .

The author with co-worker and friend, Mori-san. Tokyo, 1986.

Happy Toilet Day

I had been a copy writer at the agency for several months, my clients including Shiseido, Japan's leading pharmaceutical and cosmetic company, Bridgestone Tires and De Beers Diamonds. One afternoon, the American Creative Vice President dropped by my cubicle to ask if I'd like to teach some basic conversational English to some of the creative team—art directors, copywriters, and assistants. Since most of this staff regularly met with western clients in an attempt to sell their concepts, they were in dire need of some English language skills.

Although English is mandatory in Tokyo schools, it is taught by natives, and covers only reading and writing. Thus many students are technically literate, but the ability to converse is lacking. Anyone who happens to be bilingual is a sought-after commodity.

I agreed to hold classes three days a week during our lunch hour, happy to increase the amount of my paycheck, which was already quite hefty given the value of yen to dollar at the time.

Speaking very little Japanese, these hour-long sessions proved challenging, rewarding and often quite entertaining. And as was their custom, my students lavished me with gifts, poems, drawings and food.

Occasionally I was treated to a homemade, beautifully prepared "bento box"—a small, portable, lacquered container used to carry and serve a meal. Not just any meal, but a feast for both eyes and stomach. The Japanese meal has always been a work of art, especially compared to the mess of fast food Americans tend to wolf down while on the go.

I liked to observe my Asian friends partaking in their midday meal. Sato-san, my boss, would spread an elegant, silk-screened tablecloth across her desktop, making a ceremony out of arranging her bento box, chopsticks and green tea. Given how dignified the meal tended to be, I was always taken aback when a diner enthusiastically slurped noodles, soup or tea, a custom I came to realize is not only acceptable but a polite sign of satisfaction and appreciation for the meal.

A most curious custom I discovered involved relieving oneself in the restroom. I eventually learned that noise in the bathroom was more offensive than loudly burping, plopping your feet up on the dinner table, or blatantly picking your nose in public, which, by the way, seemed quite acceptable judging from many of the men in my office.

In addition to cleanliness, the Japanese seemed obsessed with the toilet. In fact, the Japan Toilet Association celebrates "Toilet Day" on November 10th each year. They claim the numbers eleven and ten (representing month and day) can be read as Japanese symbols for "Good Toilet." And the more elaborate the loo, the more to celebrate. In addition to taking care of waste, the top toilets offer some impressive features; they can warm, wash and deodorize. A more expensive model offers soothing music to help relax the sphincter muscles.

My first lesson in bathroom etiquette presented itself upon entering a busy women's restroom in Takashimaya, a popular department store in the trendy Ginza area of Tokyo. I noticed that while in the stall, I heard continuous flushing in adjacent stalls. Believing the commodes must be malfunctioning, I inquired later with a Japanese coworker.

"We flush many times so noise in toilet is not heard by others," she explained in all seriousness.

"This very bad manners for people in our country, especially women."

I soon discovered that although my boss Sato might have been a sophisticated diner, she was far from being a perfect lady. One afternoon while I was discussing an ad campaign with a Creative Director who was a friend, he suddenly popped a question.

"Nan-san, do you like Sato-san?"

Without much thought I replied, "Yes, of course. She is a great boss and I have learned a lot from her. Why do you ask?"

At which point he grimaced and squirmed in his chair.

"Well, most of us Japanese do not like her. We hear she makes loud noises on the toilet. We do not respect this."

Shocked by his blunt inquiry, at least I had already been informed about this disreputable breach of manners and understood its significance. I tried to find an excuse for my boss's shortcoming, and decided since she was working for an American company she figured "anything goes" in the restroom, following the "When in Rome" school of thought.

Several years after leaving Japan, we learned that our innovative Japanese friends had invented a small device that mimics the bubbling, gushing sound of a flushing toilet, with the simple push of a button. One might surmise this clever gadget not only saves water but countless reputations. It is proudly called "Sound Princess."

Translating Tragedy

Of all places, I found myself pregnant in Tokyo.

I began talking to other expectant mothers from western countries also residing in Japan, and decided upon using a female physician by the name of Doctor Morita to guide me through this nine-month adventure. She seemed to be popular and fairly well respected amongst foreigners.

I made my first appointment with this tiny, middle-aged Japanese woman and was a bit surprised at how poorly she spoke English. I convinced myself that with all my newly acquired reference books on pregnancy and childbirth, I could get through this life-altering ordeal on my own, with a little help from the good doctor.

Fortunately, I experienced a fairly easy, smooth nine months "with child" and eventually became rather fond of Dr. Morita despite our communication problems. One day when I was about four months along, I began feeling significant cramps while swimming laps at the Tokyo American Club, as was my daily exercise throughout the summer months. Alarmed, I located a pay phone near the pool, dropped in the required yen, and dialed my doctor. Choosing my words carefully, I slowly described my symptoms, followed by nerve-wracking silence from the other end of the line.

After what seemed like forever, the doctor replied, "Yes, Missus Kilmer, this might be *tragedy*. Now go to your bed, then come see me tomorrow morning and we will find your problems."

I tried to ease my panic by convincing myself that *tragedy* was not the best translation of my dilemma, and probably just meant little more than problem to my foreign doctor.

"Everything is going to be fine," I tried to reassure myself. Fortunately, I was right.

I decided it was in my best interest to join some sort of support group for expectant mothers, so I checked the local English newspapers for possible help. I first tried a "Baby Love" gathering of pregnant moms and was rather put off by the leader of the group, a spacey Australian woman named Fawn, with underarm hair longer than that on her head and a ring through her navel. She urged us to deliver our babies in the bathtub at home, under water. Fawn also insisted we save the placenta after giving birth. We were instructed to dry and preserve the organ, then brew what she claimed was an incomparably nutritious, delicious tea.

The next group I tried, Caring—Sharing—Preparing, was more my style. Founded by a knowledgeable and devoted German woman named Anke, her eight sessions, following the famous *Lamaze* childbirth method, left me feeling confident and well prepared for giving birth. I made some of my closest friends in Tokyo while enrolled in these weekly classes. Fortunately, Anke believed in an old-fashioned hospital, physician-attended delivery on dry land, followed by tossing out the placenta. And you can bet any tea she might recommend would be Twinings or another familiar brand.

Further along in my pregnancy, approaching my due date, Dr. Morita suggested an ultrasound. She wanted a final check of the fetus, to see if I was "A plus OK," in her words, for the delivery.

After the procedure, as I waited outside her examining room, the doctor suddenly ripped back the privacy curtain looking slightly horrified, and asked me, as if in disbelief, "Does husband have BIG head?"

"What do you mean? I think it is a normal size," I answered, baffled.

"Your baby have biggest head I see in long time. Could be difficult delivery."

Rather than the excruciating pain I might be facing, I immediately thought of an affliction I had read about; *Water on the Brain*.

Tears flooded my eyes and I quickly darted out of the doctor's office.

I was suddenly obsessed with measuring Japanese babies' heads. Not actually encircling their tiny skulls with a measuring tape; rather, I sized them up from across a jammed subway car, where they nestled in their mother's kangaroo pouch. Or in their prams on the crowded city streets, or in the doctor's office waiting for their next well-baby check-up.

At home, I grabbed my *Merck Manual of Diagnosis and Therapy*, a physician's reference guide I'd purchased the last time I'd been home in the states. I quickly flipped through the index pages in the back, running my finger up and down the columns until I came to the subject:

"Brain, water on," p.2223.

Even though I had read about this defect, in this moment of panic I could not think of the medical term for a kid with a big head, swollen by excessive fluid drowning the brain.

Suddenly it came to me. *Hydrocephalus*, one of a large group of genetic disorders resulting from the interaction of many genes with other genes or with environmental factors. And the leading cause of abnormally large heads in neonates.

Other grim diagnoses included cysts or tumors on the brain.

I forced a deep breath, and closed the heavy book.

For several nights I dreamed of tiny pink infants with bulging eyes and heads so heavy their bodies tumbled over and over, somersaulting. Then even tinier brown babies floated across my mental screen, their little heads barely wide enough for the two creases they called eyes.

All these tiny creatures drowned in their own bodily fluids by morning, leaving me awake, traumatized and exhausted.

I replayed over and over in my mind the conversation with Dr. Morita as to the size of my baby's father's head. It did not really matter exactly what she said; the real meaning was lost in translation.

But what was wrong with the child inside me?

Having a baby in Japan was one thing. Having a baby in Japan with water on its brain was quite another.

After a few torturous days I was relieved to learn from a British physician friend that Japanese babies have comparatively smaller heads at birth than Western babies, and that mine was most likely normal. What I really should have been worried about were the labor pains I would inevitably endure delivering an infant with such a large noggin, and with no anesthesia, as I had demanded in my ignorance.

Our daughter arrived almost two weeks after her due date. Dr. Morita had warned me that if I had gone another day without signs of labor, she would stuff my birth canal with rods of natural seaweed to get things moving. I did not look forward to this questionable procedure, to put it mildly.

This issue was one I had not read about in *What to Expect when you are Expecting*. But apparently even some OB/GYN practitioners in the western world believe that as seaweed is inserted into the moist birth canal, the plant expands to dilate the cervix and induce labor.

To my relief, I slipped into labor naturally the next morning around four, an ordeal that would end up subjecting me to nearly eighteen excruciating hours. I quickly headed to Aiku Hospital for Women, where I was scheduled to deliver my baby, if all went as planned.

Japanese doctors are reluctant to give any type of pain medication. But believing I had an exceptionally high tolerance for pain, I had informed my doctor beforehand. "No medication, no problem. I want our baby to be born naturally and free of any drugs."

After nearly twelve hours of agony, I was convinced I was going to die and all the effort and pain would have been in vain as I would never meet my firstborn child. I could hear my husband pleading with the attending nurse, "Maybe we should give her something for this pain?"

"OH NO!" The snippy nurse hissed. "Woman must not show weak face!"

Our precious, overdue daughter arrived just after nine in the evening on Friday the thirteenth, 1987, one of the luckiest days of my life. I was more than grateful to have lived to welcome her, large head and all.

We had a perfect, seven and a half pound baby girl to show for all the effort. The only foreign infant in the nursery, she was a standout amongst the tiny bundles. Hospital authorities insisted each mother get up every two hours in the middle of the night, whether the baby was awake or not. This struck me as ludicrous and cruel. But the rules, and there were many, stated that all new mothers MUST proceed at the same time to the feeding room, regardless. Each patient was to present at the nursery window, provide her infant's bassinet number, and be handed a bundle, awake, hungry or not.

I noticed the pediatric nurses casually tossed the nimble babies around. This reassured me, so fearful I was of unintentionally harming my precious newborn.

When it came my turn at the baby window no words needed to be exchanged. My baby's wispy blonde hair, fair pink skin and round, blue eyes were a dead giveaway amongst the bevy of tiny brown, slit-eyed babies topped with jet black hair.

Not to mention her humongous head.

So every few hours, a bunch of us new moms sat around in a circle in a glass enclosed room, our babies clinging to our nipples. I tried to ignore hospital visitors as they pretended not to gawk through the glass at the *gaigin* mother and her baby with the big head. Fellow nursing mothers watched me, their eyes peering over white surgical masks as I lovingly fed my newborn. Glancing up now and then, I'd catch heads snapping the other way.

Once released from the hospital, our new little family piled into a taxi headed to our Japanese home. We were eager to settle in and share our news with family and friends around the world. Little did we know what lay ahead for us in "The Land of the Rising Sun . . ."

Brittle

Sometimes, when you least expect it, life throws you a hard punch.

"Newborn babies' bones are very pliable and are difficult to break; most fractures in childhood occur after the age of two. If a fracture is suspected in an infant, abuse should be considered."

—*The Merck Manual*/Fourteenth Edition

Although by nature an obsessive, anxious worry wart, I never imagined anyone would intentionally harm my newborn child.

"Baby Caits" as we call our tiny addition, is three months old and thriving. We have just returned from a weekend in Bangkok, where we have searched for housing, as we are soon to be transferred to that exotic city where, having visited, we never wanted to live.

On this afternoon I must go into my office to present some copy I have written for a client, Shiseido. I always dread leaving my new baby for any length of time, but I feel obligated to finalize my work before leaving the country.

For several months we have been employing a young woman from Germany, Ingrid, who is a trained nurse. She babysits for us two or three times a week when I have to be at the agency.

She has been recommended to me by a friend and fellow expat, a physician herself. I feel comfortable knowing our daughter is in the good hands of a professional nanny.

It is a typically muggy summer afternoon in Tokyo when I arrive home from work and from outside the gate, I hear my baby screaming. Hurrying inside to calm her, I see Ingrid, the nanny, seated at the kitchen table reading. When she hears me, she jumps up, nervously explaining, "The baby has been crying the entire time you were out. I tried to comfort her, but I think she must be teething, so I put her down for a nap."

"I doubt she is getting teeth at three months," I disagree. "I hope she did not pick up a stomach bug while we were in Thailand."

Instantly, I bound up the stairs to calm my distressed baby. I find her swaddled in her wicker bassinet; her face is heated to a bright crimson as she wails.

Caitlin's tiny body quivers as she cries throughout the long night, alternating between piercing screams and soft weeping, so exhausted is the infant, not to mention her parents. Between my frantic husband and me, there seems to be nothing we can do to soothe this wailing child.

I carry the baby from our bed downstairs to the sofa in the living room, where I sit with her over my knee, trying to bounce away the gassy pains I believe might be jabbing at her tiny tummy.

What else could it be?

First thing in the morning I call for an appointment with her pediatrician, and I am in his office within an hour.

"My baby has been crying since yesterday afternoon, and I see no signs of any teeth coming through," I reply when asked, in broken English, why I have brought her to see the doctor.

I then add that we had been in Thailand several days earlier, and wonder if maybe she had caught an intestinal bug while there.

As I ramble, the doctor pushes and pokes at the infant, taking her temperature and listening to her heartbeat. He removes her pajama top and suddenly I notice some pale black and blue spots and slight swelling in her left arm.

Shocked beyond words I look to the doctor for some explanation.

"Was baby with other people the day before?" he asks with concern.

"Yes, yes," I babble nervously. "She was with a babysitter for a few hours, while I went to work."

"You know this person before?" His probing continues.

Growing more terrified by the moment, I feel my defenses kicking in.

"Yes, she is a young German woman who has been working for me and several of my friends for a few months; she is a trained nurse and has been highly recommended."

"I think the baby's left arm has a break. You must take her to St. Luke's Hospital in Shinjuku for x-ray."

"How can this be possible?" The words tumble from my mouth as I cry in disbelief. "No, no!"

"I do not know, but this why you must make x-ray" he tries to console me.

With that, the doctor gently wraps her swollen little arm in a bandage and wishes me well.

I first call my husband at his office who, in disbelief after hearing the doctor's report, agrees to meet me at the hospital emergency room. Next, I call my physician friend Holly, who happens to be a radiologist. She immediately comes to the doctor's office and together we hail a cab for the hospital.

Once in the emergency room, the doctors wheel the fussing infant away on a table, leaving the three of us, my husband, myself and Holly, sitting on stark wooden benches lining the long hallway. People stare shamelessly at us three visibly shaken foreigners. I sob uncontrollably while my husband and Holly try to comfort me.

After what seems like hours, the doctor returns with Caitlin, still crying uncontrollably and frightened by all the strangers and commotion. As I hold her in my arms the doctor asks us to come into his office. Holding up an x-ray, he comments.

"Yes, I am afraid the baby's left arm has been fractured at the elbow and it is quite severe. Our concern is that her growth plate has been affected, but we cannot determine this until she is at least one year old."

As he speaks, Holly carefully examines the x-ray, which is like reading Arabic for me.

I notice the doctor pulls another film from the envelope.

"Also, it appears the right arm has a fracture—not nearly as serious, just a 'greenstick' which is extraordinary for such a young baby. Usually we see this in older children, who fall while running or riding a bicycle, and try to catch themselves when they hit the ground. I cannot explain how this might have happened."

"Can this possibly get any worse?" I think to myself.

"If the growth plate is affected, what would that mean?" I ask the doctor.

"If so, then your daughter might have one arm longer than the other," he explains. I shoot an alarmed look at Holly and she sadly shakes her head in agreement.

"Isn't there anything that can be done now?" My husband desperately wants to know.

"Well, today we can set the arms as best we can, trying at all costs to avoid surgery on that left limb. Later, when she is about ten years old, she can have surgery to correct any deformity."

Deformity. The word hits my gut like a sledge hammer.

What I remember after that is foggy. I do know that before they cast both her arms, it was necessary for us to sign a release should they have to make an incision and put our baby under anesthesia. I am forever grateful that Holly was with us that horrific day, as neither my husband nor I was in any condition to think clearly while making crucial decisions.

Again, "Baby Caits" is whisked away and we wait. Outside the operating room I hear her shrill cries off and on and long to comfort her. After another agonizing hour the doors spring open delivering our beloved baby to us, white plaster casts harnessing her tiny pink, pudgy arms.

It soothes me to notice she looks more content than she has since the previous afternoon when I had left her with the nanny. She coos and grins as she sees her mommy and daddy standing over her.

"Fortunately," her doctor seems relieved to report, "we did not have to put your child to sleep. We were able to set her left arm without surgery. The right arm is a simple greenstick fracture and should heal within weeks. The left arm will take longer, and as I said, we won't know the full extent of the damage until she is at least a year old, when we can determine if her growth plate has been affected."

Gazing down at our beautiful baby girl in cumbersome casts, I smile through my tears. I have to believe she will be all right. Though I still don't believe what has happened.

The doctor decides Caitlin should spend the night at the hospital for observation and pain medication as needed. Alarmed by my appearance and concerned about my state of mind, my husband offers to stay with her in the nursery, which is a large room lined up and down with cribs full of ailing babies whom I can only hope are not contagious.

Once home, I fall into bed in my clothes and plunge into a deep sleep, beyond exhaustion. When I return to the hospital first thing in the morning, a kind Japanese nurse looks at me saying, "I do not know you! You look like different woman today!"

I fake a smile and hurry off to the pediatric ward.

There, I find my baby and her dad in good spirits; she is bobbing in his lap, cooing happily. Her heavy arms do not seem to bother her. We wait for the doctor to make his morning rounds and are ecstatic when he says the infant is doing well and can leave. As he bids us farewell he looks into my eyes.

"Your baby has so much growing to do; I am quite sure she will be fine by the time she is finished. Please do not worry, Mrs. Baker." He bows, then touches my arm ever so lightly, a highly unusual gesture for a Japanese man, especially with a western woman. I will never forget his kindness.

Back home, and with little more than a week left before our belongings are to be shipped off to Thailand, I wander around the house in a daze. In between caring for a new baby, sorting and packing, and bidding farewells to friends, we must deal with Ingrid.

It seems strange now but somehow we did not want to believe the woman had intentionally harmed our precious baby. Initially, we told ourselves it had to be an accident. Nonetheless, we had to confront her and make her explain.

A few days after Caitlin is home from the hospital, we have only begun to process what has happened. I call Ingrid's number and find her at home.

"Ingrid, this is Mrs. Baker. You have to tell me exactly what happened last Thursday when you were caring for our baby."

"As I told you, Mrs. Baker, she was crying all the time so I thought she was teething."

"Ingrid! Our baby was taken to the hospital with two broken arms!" I shrieked. "Tell me what happened! Please, tell me what happened!"

In tears at this point, Ingrid admits to me that the baby had been sitting in her carrier chair on the kitchen counter and it had slipped off, hurling her to the floor. She then offers to pay the medical bills for Caitlin's treatment.

"Money is not what we need, Ingrid," my husband interjects. "We need to know the truth. We have spoken to several pediatric orthopedic specialists in the states, and they do not believe a mere fall could break an infant's soft bones. This was not an accident. Am I right?"

"I am so very sorry," she sobs. "I did not do it on purpose. She fell. She fell from the kitchen counter."

All I want to do is get off the telephone with the woman. But I insist she come and see for herself our baby's condition. I want to witness the look in her eyes when she sees our innocent three-month-old child bound in heavy casts.

Ingrid promises to come by our house the following evening, after sitting for a family I do not know. This is when it hits me that all of her employers should be informed of what happened while she worked for us. I call everyone I know who has employed Ingrid, and they in turn call those I don't know, to spread the word about the German nanny.

Most people are as shocked as I am, having perceived the woman to be a kind and loving caregiver. The woman most upset is the mother of a young son with Down's syndrome.

"I don't know if I can get by without her," she tells me. "I have two other children and I desperately need her help."

"It is your choice," I reply. "But if what we believe is true and the woman is unbalanced and lost her temper with my child, who knows when it might happen again. And the outcome could be even worse."

As promised, Ingrid stops by the next night and I escort her into our living room. Caitlin is there swinging happily from her jump seat, her arms bound like a tiny mummy. At the sight of her former nanny Caitlin begins to cry, which haunts me. Ingrid, crying as well, touches her head affectionately and I cringe, wanting to slap her hand away.

Reaching into her purse, Ingrid pulls out an envelope and hands it to my husband.

"This is all my savings from working here in Tokyo; please take it."

"Listen, I told you, we do not want your money, Ingrid," my husband responds, struggling to remain calm. "Take it and buy an airline ticket out of the country, or we will report you to the authorities."

His command is not totally out of anger or revenge but because we honestly do not want anyone else here in Japan to go through the trauma we are experiencing. And again, we still do not want to believe anyone could intentionally hurt our child.

Ingrid announces, "Already most people I work for have fired me and told me to leave, so I have little work here now. I plan to go back to Germany as soon as I have my business in order here."

"Goodbye, Ingrid," I say out of decency and to get her out of our home. "And please get some professional help, I think you need it."

I guide her to the door, noticing she does not look back at our baby.

And we never see her again.

Thai Ties

"What a nice place to visit, but I certainly would not want to live here." This is how I'd described Bangkok after our earlier visit. The city seemed congested, polluted, and a difficult place to stay for very long.

Regardless, we are moving into our house in Bangkok, no longer visitors. Wounded, frazzled, yet determined to forge onwards, I am sitting on the floor amidst a deluge of huge cardboard boxes in the enormous, glass-walled living room of what is to be our home. Outside, Jubjee our pool boy dutifully sweeps the concrete pool deck of fallen pink and white orchid petals, palm branches and gecko poop. I am cuddling our three-month-old-daughter, who still swings around clumsy, white plaster casts on both tiny arms.

Jubjee tries not to stare at these strange new Americans with a baby who has somehow been injured. In fact, everywhere I take my baby in this new, foreign place strangers stare at us.

I grow weary of answering, "Oh my, what happened to her?"

Our household staff in Thailand consists of two maids who call themselves "Number One" and "Number Two" in order of seniority. Ranking is based upon experience, age, cooking skills and language ability. Often a "Number Two" has just come down from the hill country having never laid eyes on a foreigner nor used an indoor toilet. And a "Number One" maid might have been in town six months, learned a few basic American dishes like fried chicken and hamburger casserole, and has picked up pleasing phrases like "Mr. look very nice today," and "Madam like me to clean more?" Admittedly, we pay less than 200 U.S. dollars per month for this live-in help, so cannot complain too bitterly for their shortcomings, and there are many.

We also employ the pool boy Jubjee, whom we share with our next-door neighbors across the sprawling deck, a likable American couple in Thailand with an international shipping company. Muscular, smiling Jubjee, multi-talented and a former Thai boxer, doubles as their driver.

Our personal driver is Dang, a little, puffy, old Thai man with thinning hair dyed black as construction paper. It is nearly impossible to tell if or when his eyes are open. I like to call him our "Thai Mr. Magoo." Hopeful that his eyes are in fact open while he drives us around town, we creep along through the city's gridlocked traffic. Our driver rarely says much other than "Yeth, Madam," "No, Madam," or maybe "Where going?"

Dang's job, in my open eyes, is a cushy one. He arrives around 7:30 weekday mornings and drives "Mister" to work at Esso Thailand, some five miles away. He then returns to the house, sprawls himself on a metal folding chair outside our back door with his feet propped on the back steps, and dozes throughout the day in front of a humming fan. That is, until I might need him to drive me to Villa, the supermarket frequented by westerners in search of coveted items like wildly expensive Oreos, Cheerios, Pampers or some other American product we can't live without.

Of course, there are all the other necessary provisions, many locally produced, but the store is renowned for scoring shipments of precious goods from the west--and for being a warzone of a commercial establishment. One day I might tear the strap of my new leather sandal on a piece of metal protruding from the bread rack, another I might bump my forehead on a wooden box jutting out above the canned goods aisle. But in the end, the entire shopping trip is usually worth it, if only to see the delight on my family's faces when I present a treat like a batch of Betty Crocker brownies for dessert one evening--a little taste of home.

Dang also is on call to drive me to doctor appointments, play groups for the baby or maybe the Bangkok Polo Club for aerobics class, a swim or some tennis. I also frequent many of the open markets and endless rows of specialty stores in a city renowned for shopping. Textiles, jewels, baskets, silver, custom made clothing, hand crafted wood furniture—you name it, Bangkok has it to offer, and at bargain prices.

If all this is sounding decadent and exotic, I am not without challenges as I speak no Thai and the servants speaks little or no English. If we communicate, we point or use sign language and tasks often end up more troublesome than if I'd simply done them myself.

It does not take long to figure out that 1) Thai people do not say "No" even when it is the honest and correct answer. And 2) these gentle people consider it a sign of weakness to ask a question.

So we foresee definite problems dealing with our new household staff.

A typical Thai outdoor food stand sits outside the gate of our compound, which consists of four large, white stucco, western style houses and two large swimming pools. Chatty little men, and plump women in colorful garb stand over an open fire cooking mysterious-looking meats, vegetables, noodles, rice and locally grown peppers so hot our eyes water from ten feet away. To say Thais like spicy food is an understatement.

I might mention that as we entered the compound for our first visit, I noticed a little blonde, presumably American girl, about a year old, munching away at the stall with maids gathered around her. I was horrified at the sight of possibly rabid dogs nipping at the ankles of the sarong-clad woman bouncing the baby on her lap as she fed her some sort of reddish noodle dish with her fingers.

Mental note: First order for our maids is "NEVER TAKE OUR BABY TO EAT AT OUTDOOR FOOD STANDS!"

In addition to "That Damn Dang" as we jokingly refer to our driver, and Jubjee the peeping pool boy, we hire Dow as our "Number One" maid and Boongon as "Number Two." Actually we inherit this dynamic duo from the American family preceding us in the house, figuring this is as good a reference as any.

It is a matter of weeks before I am en route home with Dang

from a shopping trip, and passing the food stall outside our gate I spot little Caitlin perched on Dow's knee, munching on some sort of questionable meat on a stick. This is only the beginning of broken rules, and within a few months will lead to the end of the defiant maid's position with us.

Life in Bangkok as an expat is full of minor disturbances and petty annoyances. On a more serious note, there are the snakes that populate Thailand, numerous and poisonous. Early on, we visit the Bangkok Snake Farm partly out of curiosity and in an effort to desensitize ourselves to these scary creatures. Not that my fear of snakes is anywhere near my terror of birds, but I don't care for them and certainly don't like the thought of them slinking around my home.

Thailand has more than their share of snakes, and this farm is set up to produce anti-venom serum for snakebite victims around the world. Ninety percent of the country's snakes are poisonous, so chances are if you are unlucky enough to be bitten while in Thailand, you need to pay an emergency visit to the snake farm for treatment.

Located within the Thai Red Cross Unit in central Bangkok, the Snake Farm, or "Queen Saowapha Memorial Institute," is a popular tourist attraction. Trained staff grab a slippery critter out of the deep pit where they live, holding it from either side of its head. They firmly squeeze until the snake opens its mouth, revealing sharp fangs and a long, bright pink tongue darting in and out of its mouth. The venom glands then burst, emitting a thick milky fluid into a Petri dish. The precious serum is stored in labeled vials awaiting treatment for some poor victim of the donor's potentially lethal bite.

The sight is creepy, yet mesmerizing; I only hope I never need to be injected with the secretion of one of these captive villains. What's more, we later learned that some eighty King Cobras were stolen from the farm, and Thai police suspected they were sold to restaurants around town. Supposedly, wealthy Japanese and Korean clientele love eating succulent snake meat while sipping its blood; they consider the fare an aphrodisiac. This does not surprise me as I remember a co-worker in Japan being offered a snake blood potion while dining at a fancy Tokyo establishment, promising the sanguine fluid would leave him virile as a stallion.

Upon leaving the farm, my husband points out several stands along the side of the street with dead, shriveled snakes hanging from wires strung overhead. The shelves are lined with small cocktail glasses. Dang roughly translates the sign over one stand, "miracle snake blood for sale, forty baht." So, a full glass of this magic costs about two U.S. dollars.

I am sure this is a bargain, but I pass.

Headed up to bed one night, I shuffle through the glass enclosed living room towards the staircase. Glancing out at the pool deck I see a large, black garden hose draped across the sizzling concrete. Believing Jubjee has forgotten to wrap the hose and return it to the pool house, I approach the window for a closer look. At this point the elongated tube slithers toward the sliding glass door and I jump a foot off the floor. I immediately phone Elaine, the neighbor across the pool, as Jubjee and his family reside in quarters outside her back door. In no time the muscle-bound former Thai boxer appears with a garden shovel, and hacks the humongous snake into two parts, scarlet blood gushing across the steamy pavement. Without further ado, Jubjee tosses both parts of the victim into a large trash bag, fetches the real garden hose, flushes the bloody mess into the adjacent garden bed, tosses the garbage bag into the dumpster, and retreats to his tiny cubicle. He acts as if it is all in a night's work.

Another uninvited guest in our new home is the ubiquitous gecko. I realize even before we have permanently moved to the country that this tiny, harmless lizard will be a permanent resident. We had been invited to dinner at an expat home while visiting Bangkok on our house-hunting tour, and noticed during dinner a half dozen or so geckos flitting around the perimeter of the ceiling throughout our meal. I was mildly horrified as I tensely waited for a slimy greenish critter to fall onto my head or into my plate as we enjoyed an otherwise tasty Thai meal.

One Christmas while living in Bangkok, we travel home to Westchester, New York to visit the in-laws, arriving with three or four bags of our belongings along with gifts for the relatives. One morning my brother-in-law comes bolting down the stairs where most of the family sits talking over coffee in the kitchen.

"There's a weird little lizard in my bed!" he exclaims. "I have never seen one like it!"

Instantly we realize we have transported a Thai gecko across the Pacific Ocean, the United States, half way around the world--and it has lived to visit New York and our family.

Besides our gecko friends in Bangkok, we live with massive mosquitoes, giant cockroaches, rabid dogs and mangy cats.

Roosters loitering behind our house wake us most mornings with the same "cock-a-doodle-do" we recognize from home. With the honking elephants lumbering up and down the lane in front of our house, in more ways than one we often feel we are living in a circus.

Before long, the tragic event in Tokyo begins to catch up with me. I compare the sensation to the "Tilt-a-Whirl" at the Idaho State Fair in Boise, where Melody Rose and I would make ourselves sick every summer before hopping back in line for more of the nauseating thrill. Now I discover I can get the same sensation without paying for it. The room starts to spin, my stomach flips, extremities tingle, and I might throw up. I enter into a realm of otherworldliness and lose focus. On the carnival ride of life, this is but another dreaded anxiety attack catching me off guard. Or maybe I am simply experiencing a massive heart attack and will die any minute. It is hard to tell. I have tried to repress the trauma of my baby's broken arms during that discombobulating move to Bangkok, and in doing so have ignited an explosive battery of anxiety-related issues.

Desperate, I pay my first visit to nearby Samitivej Hospital, one of the largest and most respected medical facilities in Southeast Asia at the time, where most local doctors maintain offices for seeing and treating patients. I have an appointment with a Thai female general physician who has been recommended by a fellow expat neighbor. The moment I tell the well-intentioned doctor of my excessive thirst during these frequent episodes of anxiety she has me tested for adult-onset diabetes. The results are negative.

The doctor next asks for more symptoms of my discomfort. The following are the notes the woman gives me after my visit to her office in July, 1987:

"Yesterday after dinner she get diarrhea 3 times. No ab cramps or vomit. Also a strange semulation of her arms, feel weak, num. Today better no fever.

> *Got a baby 17 weeks ago.*
>
> *Severe reaction to insect bite—bee?*
>
> *PE: Not Pale BP 120/70*
>
> *COR—reg rhythm*
>
> *Pulm-clear*
>
> *Ab-soft* (Here I say hey! I just had a baby!)
>
> *NO tenderness*
>
> *Food poison? Allergy?*
>
> *No Medication for her today.*
>
> *Observe."*

The following report was written a week later, after my follow-up appointment with the same doctor:

> *"Is going on with above attacts. Palpitations, flushy skin, numbness of hands, attacts every 3 day.*
>
> *Has been under stress lately. Drinks lots of water during attack but not otherwise.*
>
> *No fever."*
>
> *Here she repeats all the body stats but adds at bottom of report:*
>
> *"Psychological problems?"*

She prescribes halcyon for nighttime.

Not a pill popper, I head home and flush them down the toilet.

Time and the distraction of having a new baby in a foreign country with a house full of strangers posing as help gets me through this rocky time. Slowly, we settle into a semblance of a daily routine in our sprawling new house in Bangkok. Thoughtful, caring neighbors and new friends help with the bumpy transition. Although I will never come to claim to thoroughly enjoy life in Thailand, surely there are worse places to call home.

Healing Factors

Around nine months after the horrific incident, we have settled into our new home in Bangkok. At this point we decide to travel home to the states, so that Caitlin can be seen by several specialists on the east coast. By now her casts have been removed and her right arm is back to "normal." Her left arm is bowed and when she crawls about it collapses into a "V" shape, though this does not seem to hold her back. She is an obliviously active, bright, happy baby girl.

In talking with various doctors in the U.S., the issue of abuse and Children's Protective Services inevitably arises. Each points out that had we been in the states and presented our child with broken bones, the authorities would have been called in immediately to interrogate us in attempt to determine the cause of the injuries.

The fact that we escaped this examination by living abroad was of little consolation to us, although I pity all the innocent parents who must face questioning about possible abuse in such heart- breaking situations.

The first orthopedic surgeon we consult practices at Einstein Medical Center in New York. Within minutes of examining her, the older, rather harsh doctor bluntly announces, "The child will require surgery before the age of ten. Being a girl it is even more important that she not be deformed. She will have about a six-inch scar down the outside of her arm but otherwise it will look fine and function well. Fortunately, she seems to have full extension of the arm so my guess is her growth plate has escaped injury."

This cold physician's manner and proposed treatment are unacceptable to us.

It is several doctors later while at Johns Hopkins hospital in Baltimore that we find a specialist who tells us what we want to hear. A renowned children's orthopedic surgeon, his office is full of pitiful young boys and girls in much worse shape than our baby. We see so many sad, possibly hopeless cases that for the first time in quite a while we feel fortunate. Our little Baby Caits is as happy and healthy as one could ask, and not aware that anything might be wrong with her.

Dr. Paul Sponseller turns out to be our hero. After studying her x-rays and examining her arms, he is more than ninety percent certain that her case was not an accident. More importantly, he promises us that by the time she is a teenager the injury will not be noticeable, except perhaps to a specialist like himself and only if it were pointed out to him.

In the doctor's words, which we cling to, "Mother Nature will take over and the girl's bones will adjust as they grow. Bring her back in about fifteen years and we will celebrate."

This is all we need to hear.

Maid in Thailand

Trying to convince myself basic medical care is sufficient in Bangkok and barraged with more household help than is necessary, I decide to attempt having a second child abroad. I figure I am not getting any younger and might never again have so much help around the house.

Surely, I try to assure myself, nothing major could possibly go wrong again . . .

By July of 1988 I take a positive pregnancy test and begin imagining a spunky little boy to keep his precious sister company. Subconsciously I wonder if I can ever love a child as much as I love my first, and hope for a boy to somehow balance my emotions.

My second pregnancy goes according to my trusty books and at twenty-two weeks along, I have an ultrasound performed at the local hospital. The results make me smile.

"Enlarged uterus with a single viable fetus in utero.

BPD is measured 52 mm, good proportion of the fetal head to trunk, no anomaly seen.

Femur length is 34 mm. Fetal SCROTUM and PENIS is seen. Normal placental thickness with previa totalis. Normal amount of amniotic fluid.

IMPRESSION: Unremarkable male fetus, 22 weeks in size.

Advise follow-up in third trimester."

Not only does our baby turn out to be a boy, but a normal, healthy, well-proportioned little guy—and with a normal-sized, well-proportioned head!

My one and only objection to this report . . . our son is positively remarkable. And fortunately, my pregnancy proved quite unremarkable.

I do give our faithful Thai maids credit for having made my second pregnancy a little easier. As I waddle through my less than taxing daily activities like grocery shopping, lap swimming, flower arranging, letter writing and reading, the domestic help is good for building Lego houses with Caitlin, paging through picture books with her and watching *Sesame Street* and *Clifford* tapes from home, understanding little or nothing of the childish dialogue. For the most part the toddler adores the doting women who spoil her, and realizes that with a smile she can get whatever she wants—as long as Mommy isn't looking.

There are daily ups and downs in our household in Bangkok. Since by nature Thai people are reluctant to ask questions, our ditsy maids often take matters upon themselves. One afternoon while I am upstairs playing with the baby, Boongon, in a burst of energy, decides to polish the white Formica kitchen counter tops. Rummaging through the pantry shelves, she finds a red white and blue spray can resembling many of the household cleaning agents she has used before. She cannot read English.

Grabbing the can, she thoroughly sprays down every square inch of Formica. Once the surfaces are saturated, she uses a rag to buff the counters to a glistening shine.

The kitchen sparkles and she is pleased with her work.

About the time she has finished her project, I come down to the kitchen. Placing a small glass on the counter I am surprised to watch it slide across the counter and crash onto the floor. Puzzled, I run my fingers over the surface which feels like a small oil slick. I try another counter and my hand slips and slides. It does not take me long to figure out that the dear maid has polished our kitchen with WD-40.

Weeks later we are still slipping around the kitchen as we seek to find a safe solution to remove the stubborn greasy film coating the surfaces.

"Madam, I think this make kitchen clean! Sorry!" Boongon chirps.

Just when I have almost gotten over the WD-40 incident and forgiven the clueless maid, she decides to disinfect the bathrooms. This time she chooses a large red and yellow spray can from the cleaning supply shelf in the pantry. It is the scent that gives her away when I return home that afternoon. Boongon had thoroughly scoured our tubs and toilets with a can of insect repellent.

Another day I am out with Caitlin at a BAMBI meeting—"Babies and Mothers of Bangkok International." This is a social/

educational group started by some British women to promote camaraderie amongst foreign mothers living in Thailand with small children. Meanwhile, back at the house, Boongon, in charge of laundry, pre-treats stains, washes, and dries our clothing, sheets and towels daily. In addition, she irons everything, including our underwear. This seems a bit excessive to me, but I do not argue and let her go about her business.

As it turns out, Boongon runs out of laundry detergent while I am out, and still has a large load of bath towels to wash before she is finished for the day. Not one to slack off in her duties, she searches the pantry for an alternative. She is pleasantly surprised to find a full case of bright green boxes with the word *CASCADE* written across each. Opening the box she sees what looks like detergent and is convinced this is what she needs.

Happily, the cheerful maid proceeds with her chore of laundering our new, bright red cotton towels. I have recently purchased these luxurious 100% Egyptian cotton towels while on a shopping trip to Hong Kong. They nicely match our new tropical- print shower curtain in the master bath.

I wonder what she thinks when she removes the warm, clean towels from the dryer and must notice they are no longer solid red but a tie- dyed pink and white pattern.

"Look Madam! Towels more pretty now!" Boongon gushes as my heart sinks.

Curious, I check the label of one of the dishwasher detergent boxes, and read

You get classic CASCADE CLEAN with the grease fighting power

of DAWN. Cleans so thoroughly virtually nothing is left behind but Pure Clean, Pure Shine.

I cannot imagine what harsh bleaching agents are contained in this super cleansing formula. I do cut Boongon some slack in that electric dishwashers are virtually non-existent in Thailand and she has never heard of this type of detergent. We had carried it along with us from Japan not knowing our dishwashers here would be human.

Needless to say, I begin hiding every cleaning product and/or spray can in our house—carefully rationing each only at the specific, detailed request of one of our hardworking, well intentioned maids.

After firing defiant Dow from her number one position, we replace her with a pleasant woman called Pim. This elegant maid wears colorful silk Thai sarongs which she sews herself, and is skilled at preparing delicious meals with a smile.

Practically perfect Pim is too good to be true. Before a year has passed her former employers, a British couple, return to Bangkok and offer her a higher salary than we are willing to pay. The Brits have no children and a smaller house, so Pim leaves us for the less demanding job. Neither Caitlin's winning smile and playful manner nor our baby's irresistible dimples convince the miracle maid to stay with us. Loyalty was not her strength, so maybe she wasn't perfect.

Our next hire is a pleasantly plump middle-aged woman who seems to have "been around the block" a few times and convinces us she will be the best head maid we have ever employed. Porntip is a decent cook with an especially tasty stir fry that becomes a favorite. Her English is the best we have heard from a maid in the two years we have been in Thailand. Not quite as likeable or attractive as Pim, Porntip seems a good fit for our Thai household.

Meanwhile, good old Dang remains our absent-minded, clueless driver, still sprawled outside the kitchen most days, dozing and lightly snoring in the blistering tropical heat until summoned to drive us into town. Actually, we don't know any other expat in Bangkok who has employed the same driver for their entire posting. Gambling, drinking and petty theft are common problems with the men in this profession, thus most people go through a string of chauffeurs during their stay in Thailand. Dang is our faithful chauffeur during our entire stay in his country, and we learned several years later he died of a heart attack at the age of eighty-three while driving an employer. We had no idea Dang was as old as he was or might have been a tad more nervous having him blindly drive us around town. His hair dye hid years. And I might have thought twice when after our precious son was born dear Dang drove the baby and me home from the hospital.

Porntip has been working for us for some time when our family travels back to the states for the Christmas holidays. We spend an entire month visiting relatives in New York, Washington, D.C. and Idaho. Everyone enjoys meeting our new little boy, John Preston, who is nearly a year old and crawling like a spider. J.P. is such a fun guy he does not sleep a wink during the 27 hour commute half way around the world from Bangkok to New York City. I refuse to sedate children as some suggest to make kids sleep on long flights. It would be just my luck for the medication to have the opposite effect, which can happen. J.P. is hyper enough without being drugged.

Our two maids have the month off although we have asked them to keep an eye on the house and to have it clean when we arrive home in mid-January. The two women take turns going "up country" to visit their families while we are away and promise not to leave the house unattended at any time.

We have a great home leave stateside and arrive back in Bangkok a few pounds heavier and loaded down with American supplies like Pampers, Pantene, and duty-free liquor. Flaky Boongon immediately manages to offend me with her welcome greeting.

"Madam get fat in American—right?" Livid, I later am informed that being told you've gained weight is a compliment coming from a Thai person; it means you have plenty of money, are doing well and can afford lots of good, rich food.

I immediately go on a strict diet.

The first night home we put the babies to bed and get ourselves ready for a good night's sleep after our long flight. As I head down to the kitchen for a glass of water, my husband asks, "Would you please bring me a small glass of cognac when you come up?"

Looking around the top shelf of the pantry I notice every single bottle of liquor is empty, and I am puzzled. We always have a well-stocked liquor supply, picking up a bottle or two each time we pass through the Duty-Free shop at an airport. It strikes me that the maids must have thrown quite a bash and polished off our entire liquor supply while we have been away.

"Porntip and Boongon, would you both please come in here?" I call to the maids who are in their quarters outside our kitchen.

"Yes, Madam," both women respond at once. "I come."

I notice right away that Porntip is turning pale, while Boongon, as usual, looks clueless.

"What happened to all of our liquor?"

Porntip immediately begins to sob telling me her boyfriend drank all of our alcoholic beverages. "Well," I scold her, "you will have to replace it all with your monthly pay, do you understand?"

"Yes, yes, Madam, I buy more whiskey for you and Mister."

With this, she hurries out of the house, leaving Boongon to report to me, "Madam, I see Porntip drink too much of your bottles, not boyfriend."

As it turns out, Porntip likes liquor and had taken off on a bender while we were away in the states. In the end, we fired the woman, although her boyfriend tried to tell us, "I take Porntip to temple. Evil Spirits go away. Now her head good."

We assume he is talking about an exorcism. Evil spirits or not, the woman will no longer work for our family.

Next in our line of maids comes Dok-Rak, a Thai name that we are told means "Flower of Love." Dok-Rak has worked as a head maid for another Esso family who is moving to Europe, so we inherit her from them, with decent references and few complaints. She works for us for the remainder of our time in

Thailand, which is only six months, as we are transferred back to the states the following summer. She, Boongon and Dang all sob as we depart their country. We realize the tears are not so much for me and my husband, but for our two sweet babies whom they've grown to love like their own.

I am sure the flight from Bangkok to San Francisco will never end and remind myself that this is our last trip half way around the world, at least for the time being. I seriously doubt I could endure one more twenty-four hour flight with two toddlers who seem to want to convince me they are fun-loving insomniacs.

Thai maid, Pim, holding author's 18-month-old daughter. Bangkok, 1988.

Altered States

After six years living as an expat I was eager to slave over a hot stove, scrub toilets, shuttle kids, tackle piles of laundry, and wander around the house in my underwear, even if it hadn't been ironed. I longed for *normal* things like independence and privacy, and looked forward to life back home.

Dallas would not be my choice for a new home in the states, but the decision is not mine. Our search for a house turns up a homey looking place the Cleavers might have liked, tucked away on a tree-lined street in a family friendly area known as University Park. One might think this would all feel natural and comfortable, but we are taken off guard by that curious "Reverse Culture Shock," described by experts as *"returning home after growing accustomed to a different lifestyle, customs and routine, to experience the same initial shock effects as moving away, sometimes even more intensely. This is often a repetition of anxieties and concerns and for some people can last longer than the initial jolt."*

Behavioral specialists claim it takes roughly twenty-one days to form or break a habit. Having spent six years in Asia, setting up a household as newlyweds, working in a foreign environment, and introducing two children into the world, it is surprising our eyes are still round. Then suddenly we are back in the homeland and things don't seem that familiar. Personally, I think this strangeness is exaggerated by the fact we are in Texas, a region in many ways more foreign to us northerners than any remote spot in Asia.

Our children are in awe of this new life in a country mostly strange to them. Upon realizing Americans drink tap water, Caitlin marvels, "Mommy, they drink the hand- washing water in this place!" She'd been taught in Thailand that tap water was poison.

It is little wonder my toddling son has chronic digestive problems for months once we relocate to America. His immature system is accustomed to Asian germs and he must gradually adjust to new bacteria. Everything from wearing shoes inside to sidewalks to automatic dishwashers is a novelty for him and his sister, including take-out food delivery.

One night as we unpack boxes, line shelves and hang pictures, I order dinner from a nearby restaurant. The bell rings and I head to the door, little JP pitter pattering after me—in his drooping diaper. A small, grinning Chinese man greets me holding a large brown paper bag.

"Here your food, Mam!" he proudly shoves the order in my face.

"Enjoy so much!"

"Thank you, what do I owe you?"

"Is twenty two dollar with thirty cent!" he garbles.

I pay what he's asking and grab my order.

"Thanks again and have a nice evening," I chirp as I lock the door.

The curious toddler follows me back into the kitchen looking pensive.

"What dat, Mommy?" he inquires.

"Well, kiddo, this is our dinner. That nice Chinese man brought some delicious food for us to eat. Look inside the bag."

I stoop to show him the little white cartons, familiar chopsticks and cellophane wrapped fortune cookies. He takes a quick peek, and not terribly interested in what he sees, toddles out of the room, jabbering to himself, "I wonder what flight dat man took?"

As with each of our household moves, I scramble to get the kids into a normal routine, enrolling them in preschools and playgroups and researching medical care. Their dad goes off to his new job, staff and life as a rising executive. Most days I find myself home unpacking more boxes, hammering nails into the wall, lugging furniture from room to room, scouting out the neighborhood, and staring into space, wondering where my life might be headed.

After several months trying to settle into our new home I become painfully aware that every afternoon my forehead starts to throb and my eyes feel as if they might burst out of my skull. It seems to me that each time we move, my body manifests a different symptom of stress, and now I am plagued by these reoccurring headaches. Anxiety attacks or even chronic diarrhea might be more tolerable than this steady jackhammer in my head. I am about ninety-five percent certain this latest affliction is caused by the strain of moving our family half way around the world, rather than a brain tumor or impending aneurism. Otherwise the headaches would be constant and totally debilitating, I try to reassure myself.

The pounding in my skull becomes intolerable and I make an appointment with a psychologist referred to me by my husband's employer. Let's call her Lydia. This is my second time to talk with a licensed therapist. The first time I met with a social worker in Bangkok who informed me, "My area of expertise is really philandering spouses, a common problem here in Thailand with all the prostitutes roaming the streets offering any service one might desire, so I'm not sure I can help you, dear." Hearing my story, she admitted she had never encountered a woman whose baby's bones had been intentionally broken while living in a foreign country, preparing to move to another. Like she'd told me, cheating husbands was her forte. She suggested I try a yoga class or jogging. And I paid for this advice.

The Dallas therapist is a pleasant enough woman who peers at me from behind wire-rimmed glasses. She reminds me of Hillary Clinton with her frosted bob and sensible tan pantsuit attempting to disguise hefty hips. Her office is tacky Texan with a rug shaped like the state and too many wooden plaques with inspirational sayings like "Today is the Tomorrrow You Worried about Yesterday," and "When Life gives you Lemons, make Lemonade."

Our session begins with Lydia placing a box of Kleenex on the table in front of me.

"How old are you, Nan?" she inquires, glancing at the forms I have completed in her waiting room.

Before I can answer, she blurts, "Oh my! You are over thirty? You don't look a day over twenty!"

Her flattery eases some tension in my neck and shoulders so I smile and joke, "I feel better already, thank you!"

"So tell me about the problems you are experiencing, dear. I see here you have recently moved back from Asia. Are you not a Texan?"

Wondering what difference it makes if I am a native of the state or not, I begin to describe the accident in Tokyo, challenging life in Bangkok, our taxing moves around the world, and my daily, recurring headaches. I also admit to the doctor that I have a tendency toward hypochondria, especially after reading medical books, and can convince myself I have the symptoms I read about in scientific terms. I do not mention to her that I have ruled out a brain tumor as the cause of my troublesome condition.

The woman offers an oddly sympathetic smile, then totally unnerves me.

"You know, Nan, I have a daughter about your age, and just last year she was diagnosed with a brain tumor. I want you to go directly to a physician to rule out tumors, cancer—any disease which might be precipitating your chronic headaches."

Trying to regain my composure, I inch my way out of her suffocating office while she babbles on about what might possibly be wrong with me.

I never return to find out.

Fed up with therapists, I take matters in my own hands and join the local YMCA. Concentrating on a trendy new class of madly stepping up and down on a bench, lifting weights, and jumping rope, not all at the same time, seems to relieve some of my anxiety. Plus, I meet fellow fitness buffs and begin to get to know some Texans, many of them transplants. I am amused by the typically upbeat natives who invariably declare. "Y'all just hafta come to dinner at our place, ya hear?" Even if most never did come through with a real invitation, it was fun listening to them drawl on about how great (pronounced grite) it was to meet me. And how, "Y'all are gonna just luuuuu-vvv it here in Dallas, hon!"

Pets and Pests

As our little family settled into life in "The Big D" we decided we needed a pet. Given the amount we travel, Preston had always favored what he referred to as "flushable pets." So we purchased from the local pet store a bright red little fish we called Scarlett. The slimy little swimmer lived in the kitchen in a round glass bowl filled with water and greenery, and when passing by I often found myself chatting to her. After all, I had read that these little animals are quite intelligent, and social by nature.

"Good morning, Scarlett, how's the water?" I didn't want her to feel lonely but realized it was I who was craving conversation. Smart as they might be, fish can't talk.

Scarlett ended up in the toilet after six months or so, a victim of overfeeding, I assumed, or maybe loneliness, or both. I could relate.

Though not flushable, our next pet was a fury chocolate brown rabbit we should have named Houdini rather than Tootsie. She lived in a cage in the backyard, but preferred wide open spaces and playing chase. Once let out of her cage, Tootsie's mission was to escape under the fence, so I spent much of the bunny's short life frantically chasing her around the neighborhood.

Tootsie didn't just nibble, she chewed, and when she discovered the cord of a remote controlled toy bulldozer one afternoon while hopping around in the garage, she took advantage. Chomping on the shiny black plastic coated wire like it was a root in her burrow, Tootsie devoured the three foot cord, at least that's how we believe it disappeared. Our suspicions were confirmed when later that night our elusive bunny went into cardiac arrest and died on the floor of her cage.

Tootsie had only been with us four or five months, but we felt her loss as if she were family. We held a solemn, non-denominational burial service in the yard she so loved to escape, with a tearful ceremony on our back deck. Only family and a few select friends attended, followed by cookies, lemonade and Tootsie tales. It choked me up to watch little J.P. for months as he'd pass by Tootsie's gravesite near the garage, gazing up at the heavens, little hand over his big heart.

Anyone who's been to Dallas or watched the TV show knows the city, with all its glitter and glam, has its darker side. J.R. wasn't the only bad guy in town, and as it turned out, I had dated one of them when we were teenagers back in Idaho.

The first holiday season we spent in Dallas, my parents were visiting and my mother and I were shopping in a Williams Sonoma near our house. Admiring the latest in kitchen gadgets we were approached by a familiar face I could not place for a few moments.

"Aren't you the Kilmers?"

Startled, I admitted our identities and he introduced himself as a kid we had known fairly well some twenty five years earlier back in Nampa. Rick, I will call him in an attempt to save his face a bit too late, was on the swim team with me when we were growing up. We had dated briefly while in high school but he was Mormon and we clashed on certain issues. He had always been a good looking, charming guy, and it seemed the years hadn't changed him.

Living once again in a new town where I knew no one, meeting up with someone from my past was heartening. I soon learned that Rick had married a woman from Idaho whose job brought her to Dallas, hence he followed and was working as an interior decorator.

"Perfect," I told him. "We just moved into our house and I will need some help getting things pulled together."

Rick happened to live in our neighborhood, University Park. He shared that he and his wife were divorced and he was the main caretaker for his two sons. So, I surmised, he was generous and kind-hearted as well.

For several months Rick helped me with the house, introducing me to the Decorators' Center and urging me to spend more on trendy home accessories than I intended. He explained he was renting the modest little bungalow where he was living only until his estate was complete in Highland Park, one of the more prestigious neighborhoods in the city. And as for the clunky Chevy Lumina he drove around town, this was due to the fact that he had been rear-ended in his Porsche. The prized vehicle had been in the shop for weeks when the owner went out of business and disappeared, along with the sports car. Rick simply hadn't had time to track down the shyster or purchase new wheels.

If the man had bad luck he also had a poor memory. More often than not, when he'd join us for dinner out or a movie, he'd forgotten his wallet. Or maybe misplaced it? Occasionally he'd pose as a big spender and pay for all of us, usually from a large wad of bills dug out of his coat pocket.

My nagging suspicions were confirmed when we ordered expensive, custom window treatments through Rick, who'd convinced us he'd save us money using his decorator's license. It was not until we'd paid for the blinds (using a money order at his insistence) and they never arrived that we were convinced we were dealing with a crook. At that point I threatened to contact his parents back in Idaho, so he came through with the blinds and we never heard from him again.

Several years later, I ran into one of his sons at a Dallas Cowboys game and he told me his father was in jail on drug charges and mail fraud. He offered his mother's phone number for the rest of the story, but I already knew more than enough about my old friend, the con artist.

From then on I was on extra high alert for shady characters lurking in our seemingly idyllic neighborhood. One afternoon, the kids and I headed over to NorthPark, an upscale mall nearby. I needed to pick up a suit I'd had tailored at Neiman Marcus. I assured the two youngsters it was nearly dinnertime so we wouldn't be spending much time at the mall—just a dash in to pick up the suit.

Once inside the mall the children darted over to the tall, sloping wall circling a small fountain just outside Neiman's. As they scurried over to climb part way up the wall, I gave my permission for just one slide down, their favorite activity on an otherwise boring outing. Watching them swish down the slippery stone, I noticed a nice-looking, prematurely grey, middle-aged man in khakis and a pink oxford shirt staring at them, then me. Instinctively, I grabbed the two children, urgently pulling them towards the store. The man promptly followed us, picking up his pace and getting closer than was natural. My radar ignited and I realized this was an unstable character in pursuit of me and my children. At this point we were running towards the entrance of the store, and the crazed guy began hissing at me.

"You are NOT their mother, you bitch, you know you are NOT their mother! Give me those kids!"

Clinging to my wits as best I could, I dragged the stunned children behind the cosmetics counter at the front of Neiman's and pleaded with the girl at the Lancôme display to call Security. In a wise move, she bent down to my kids' eye level and calmly asked, "Do you know this woman? Is she your mother?"

Caitlin assured her with a quivering lip. "Yes, she's our mommy, I know her really well." Meanwhile, J.P.'s grip nearly cut off circulation to my right thigh. The Lancôme lady quickly dialed Security and within seconds casual shoppers whom I later learned were undercover agents, posing as characters like a biker-looking guy in chains and a black leather jacket, fashionably dressed blonde female shopper, and tousled teen in school uniform, swarmed the first floor of the store. Someone with a badge appearing to be in charge swiftly pulled the three of us into a back office where we waited wide-eyed and shaking for the bad man to be apprehended.

"We have this store totally covered at all times, we'll catch this creep," the authority assured me.

Before long a uniformed policeman arrived to evaluate the situation. I had to honestly report that the wild man in the pink shirt and khaki pants had NOT actually touched any of us, so we learned that he could not, by law, be taken into custody. The cop escorted us out to my car, where we all bolted inside as I locked the doors and buckled us up. Barely breathing as I sped home, my eyes darted at the rearview mirror every few seconds, half expecting to spot that lunatic running after our car screaming more obscenities.

The rest of our time in Dallas, my daughter refused to shop at any mall. And it would be years before my traumatized son would walk with me in public without keeping a tight grip on my hand. The boy was twelve, possibly thirteen, when his older sister told him it was unacceptable and totally embarrassing for a teenager to hold his parent's hand in public, or even privately for that matter. The poor kid inherited his mother's skittish temperament.

Naked Joy

If you don't count running into a childhood friend turned felon, or being chased by a lunatic through the fanciest mall in town, most of our three years spent in Dallas proved pleasant, yet unremarkable. So we were not terribly disappointed to learn we would again be relocating the following summer. This next move would take us just four hours away and two hundred miles down barren Interstate 45. We'd be headed for Houston, where my husband and I had not stepped foot since leaving for Japan as childless newlyweds ten years earlier. So this fourth largest city in the U.S. was to become home once again, at least for another five years or so.

Houston appeared to be an acceptable place to raise kids if you didn't mind sticky summers that tended to obliterate spring and fall, two of my favorite seasons. Texans have a serious fondness for firearms so we were forewarned to check out the weapon supplies in homes our kids might visit. In my naiveté, it took me a while to realize we were not talking about "bang, bang, shoot em up" toys, but the real deal.

We found a home in Hunter's Creek, one of three small villages west of downtown. The kids' elementary school was just around the corner and they quickly made friends and started to become part of the neighborhood. We were surprised when Houstonians suggested dinner at their homes and actually followed through with a real invitation. They impressed us as more genuinely friendly than folks back in Dallas, with their obligatory, "Y'all gotta come over for dinner!" In Dallas, this invitation was more often than not simply hot air.

Fighting complacency while living in hot, hazy Houston, I dared myself to enroll in a summer writing course at Dartmouth College in New Hampshire. An alum, Preston had passed along information about the school's program for aspiring writers. For years I'd stored a dress box full of partially finished stories under my bed, so I decided this might be a chance to polish the tales, never stopping to consider someone might one day actually read them.

Once my acceptance to the program known as W.R.I.T.E. arrived in the mail, I panicked. I had taken enough writing courses in my time to know I was subjecting myself to criticism, rejection and humiliation. And the fact that this was an Ivy League school where my ego would be stabbed fueled my gnawing anxiety. But the family had already decided to make this a vacation; there was no turning back. While I made a fool of myself at the college, they'd rent a cozy cabin on a lake in the New Hampshire woods. I would toil away writing while they hiked, waterskied, canoed, swam and enjoyed summertime in New England.

Driving onto the campus that summer afternoon I feel myself sinking lower in the seat of the Bronco we've rented at Logan airport. Everyone sauntering across the sprawling green lawn looks so young and intelligent, like they know exactly where they are going. I wonder whatever possessed me to think I, a frumpy homemaker, could fit in here in this epitome of academia.

We park the car and I hop out to fetch my assigned dorm room key from the registrar. Once I've secured the key, I jump back into the bright red SUV. Slamming the passenger door, I do not realize I have snatched part of a towering pine tree in the doorframe, attaching it securely to our Bronco. As we drive away clusters of cool college kids stare in disbelief. We are dragging along a lower portion of a lush tree that must have been growing for a century outside the school's historic Administration building.

For years the kids will tease me by referring to this escapade as the Bakers' version of the "Griswolds Do Dartmouth."

In anticipation of the course, I have chosen from the dusty box under my bed a few true tales I would like to submit for my fellow writers to *critique*, which I presume means *rip to shreds*. "Just the Right Leg" is one I have brought along to share.

Pulling up to my assigned dorm, one of the first people I see getting out of a van is a youthful looking brunette woman with a ponytail. I first notice her gait; she is limping and I naturally assume she has been cramped up in the car for too long. Then I notice she is wearing shorts and missing her right leg. I quickly decide it might be a tad awkward if not cruel for me to read from one of my favorite pieces, the quirky childhood story about my one-legged neighbor, Claire.

What are the chances? I took this as an ominous sign of the days to come.

Required reading for my course had been a novel, *Brooklyn Boy* written by Dartmouth professor Alan Lelchuk, who would be teaching my class. Entering the opening reception that evening, I spot the author leaning against a pillar and doing a good job of resembling himself as he appears on his book's jacket. I try to act casual and confident as I stumble towards the man, bumping a tray of canapes, spilling my wine and fighting the urge to bolt out of the room. I am wondering if he might be as sleazy as the main character in his story, which I assume is loosely based on his own life. After all, he is teaching a course on memoir.

The professor is short and slight, with misbehaving, wiry silver hair, a skimpy beard and friendly blue eyes that twinkle behind oval wire-rimmed glasses. Introducing myself, I am instantly relieved when I find I am as comfortable talking with him as I might be my grandfather. He doesn't remind me in the least of Charles Manson, Jeffrey Dahmer or my creepy Uncle Elmer.

We are divided into groups of twelve or so writers and during our initial meeting with Alan, as he asked to be called, he comments, "In all my years of teaching, I notice there is often one quiet student who usually sits in the back of the class. I have learned not to overlook this individual or assume he or she has nothing to contribute. I find sometimes this turns out to be the most promising, prolific student in the room."

I find some comfort in this remark, knowing I'd undoubtedly be sitting quietly in the back of the room, though I could promise little else.

Our class is an interesting mix of characters of varying ages and backgrounds. Each of can only hope we have a unique story and we've come here in hopes of learning how best to tell it. We discuss exemplary memoirists like Mary Karr, Frank McCourt, Jill Kerr Conway and David Sedaris, a writer with whom I am not yet familiar. Later, I will be compared to Sedaris by a fellow writer, a compliment of which I am hardly worthy but will brag about whenever I get the chance.

Our daily classes are held in Sanborn Hall, which houses the English Department and sits on a corner of the sprawling grass quad, "The Green" as it's been called over the years. The moment I enter our room on the third floor I realize there is no sitting in the back here, no place to retreat and hide. Participants meet around a large, rectangular oak table that fills most of Sanborn's sun-drenched, wood paneled reading room. It also quickly becomes apparent Alan will not allow anyone to remain quiet in his class. He wants to know all about each one of us wannabes.

"Nan, what makes you want to be a writer?" he begins his probing. For lack of a better response, I answer honestly. "Oh, I don't want to be a writer; I have to be one. Does this make any sense?"

More than a few heads seated around the table nod in agreement.

"I just can't *not* write," I continued to blubber, further embarrassing myself.

Our first assignment is to write at least ten new pages to present to the group for discussion. We are not allowed to submit material previously written which throws me, as I'd hoped to use old writing as fall back. After class I head back to my dorm to sit at my computer and stare out the window until dinnertime. After dinner alone in the dining hall, I return to my room. I resume staring out the window, except now all I see is darkness. The same sinking thought haunts me until nearly midnight.

"What kind of delusional masochist am I? Even if I could write, who'd want to read it anyway?"

Morning classes are a welcome relief from the lonely, grueling hours spent each afternoon and evening, late into the night, trying to compose some decent, if not compelling work. Alan is a witty, engaging teacher who challenges us to fulfill our potential, should we have any. The talent in the room slowly reveals itself as authors present their writing; some show promise, much need work, and most make mine feel lame. It doesn't help that a sixteen-year old in our group shares her piece about an identical twin sister dying of a rare cancer that leaves most of us adults looking for a tissue, if not the door.

At the finish of class on about the fourth day, I am hustling out of the room trying to avoid any eye contact when I feel a tug on my shirt sleeve.

"Nan, will we have something from you by tomorrow, do you think? You can't make progress if you don't share, my dear. Is there anything I can do for you?"

"Not really," I fib, thinking I need so much help I would not know where to begin.

Pacing the room and reminding myself to breathe deeply, I try to fend off a full blown anxiety attack later that evening. I convince myself things have deteriorated to the point I either have to sit down and write or pack up and leave. Considering the money I have invested and the fact that I have no means of transportation and would have to hitchhike out of town, I begin writing down random thoughts about hokey little Nampa, Idaho. I slump at the keyboard throughout the night, at times laughing out loud, which I can only hope is a sign of progress, not insanity.

The next morning I arrive at class and sit in my usual place, closest to the door.

Alan seems pleased to see I have papers to distribute to the class and suggests I read first. I feel picked upon and like I might wet my pants there in front of everyone.

"Naked Joy" I manage to squeak, then clear my throat and repeat as loudly as possible.

"NAKED JOY" is the working title for my book.

The class responds with favorable sounds, chuckling and some "hmmmm"s like they actually might be concentrating on my reading. To my relief, they seem to laugh at appropriate passages, thankfully when humor is my intention. When I am finished, Alan smiles and compares my story to Thornton Wilder's "Our Town"—only better! Did he really say that? I look around the room and find others shaking their heads in agreement, so I assume I heard right. Wow. To be honest, I could barely listen to the next readings, I was so eager to get out of that classroom, regain some composure, and continue writing, bolstered by such positive feedback.

I sleep soundly that night despite my anxiety over returning to the classroom in the morning when Alan would be giving me his written evaluation. Arriving at Sanborn I reluctantly hike the creaky stairs to the third floor reading room where I find most of the class already seated. The professor is characteristically late and we all sit around discussing life in Hanover, the best happy hours, juiciest burgers and most popular jogging trails.

Alan finally shows up, cranks open the heavy door and pokes his head inside the room. He looks directly into my eyes and motions with his finger for me to come outside. From the bright, sunny classroom he lures me into the eerily dark hallway at the top of the stairs. If anyone else is out here, I am too terrified to notice. I am sure he intends to let me down gently, excuse my mediocre attempt at writing, and suggest I try painting or macramé. I focus on his face which seems to be floating in the darkness. He motions me closer. As I gasp for air, the hallway begins to close in on me and I expect to pass out at any moment.

"I must say, Nan, after all your hesitance and apparent lack of confidence in yourself, you have surprised me," he softly assures me. "You are a writer."

I swoon and want to hug the man but instead stumble backwards like a drunk, nearly falling down the stairs.

"Don't give up, my friend. You can succeed if you stick to it. Now pull yourself together; we are late for class!"

The remainder of my writing days at Dartmouth are a blur as I struggle with the terrifying proposition of being a real author. Until now, I had often felt like nothing more than a fraud posing as a writer, ready to shove my scribblings back under the bed.

The summer W.R.I.T.E. session winds down with a farewell dinner of mystery meat and sappy sentiments. All of us tormented writers wish each other luck as we bid our farewells. We vow to keep in touch, though this is doubtful in a world not yet cluttered with the likes of Facebook, Twitter or Instagram.

Plus, we all want to believe we have much better things to write.

The Spy Next Door

Having grown accustomed to a gypsy lifestyle, after six years living in Houston I found myself antsy. So when word came we were once again being relocated, I could barely conceal my excitement from die-hard Texan friends. I mean, in their minds, "Who would ever want to leave the greatest place on earth?"

Our new assignment would be taking us to Virginia, just across the river from the nation's capital. I was somewhat incredulous because this time around we'd be moving to a place I might have chosen to live myself, if ever given the chance.

The kids, less than enthusiastic, had to be convinced there was desirable life outside of Texas and their circles of friends, so the move was not to be without resistance, by any means. I could only hope my desperate bribes and optimistic attitude might convince them to look forward to yet another adventure into the unknown.

Exploring the northern Virginia suburbs, we settled on a house in Vienna, in a highly touted school district. The town struck me as a sleepy little village where life would be safe, quiet and comfortable. Though intense competition on athletic fields and in the classroom made our former life in Texas seem laid-back, the townsfolk, if not necessarily warm, were hospitable enough. After all, their state motto claims, "Virginia is for Lovers."

It didn't take me long to figure out the area where we'd settled cultivated more than the amorous. The place seemed to be crawling with spooks. I guess it only made sense when you considered the Central Intelligence Agency was tucked back in the woods just a few miles down the road, heading east towards D.C. Driving past the C.I.A. now and then, I strained to catch a glimpse of what might be going on inside, but could see nothing beyond the heavily barricaded entrance to the grounds. I sometimes found myself fantasizing that the government might be hiring locals, looking to recruit unassuming nobodies like myself.

I should not have been surprised when many of the people I met around town curiously did not seem certain about what they did for a living. When I asked, if I got an answer at all, it tended to be along these lines: "I'm with the State Department," followed by a quick change of subject.

Some friends of our children seemed equally reluctant to share. When questioned about a parent's job, these kids might answer a little too quickly, "I have no idea what my dad/mom does. I don't think they ever told me."

These were boys and girls old and sharp enough to know what their parents were up to everyday of the week. My kids would never allow us to leave them in the dark, or so I believed as my mind leapt to conclusions.

Alas, I had nothing to hide from anyone. A less than glamorous homemaker, with the husband and kids off to work and school each day, I was left to create some sort of life for myself in this new setting. Should I begin feeling lonely, bored, or simply misplaced, I'd remind myself of those times I'd longed for *normal* while living overseas all those years.

Little did I know at the time, but one of the country's most infamous counter intelligence agents was living in our neighborhood. In fact, I unknowingly drove past his house almost daily for my routine car pool, shopping or errands. The elusive spy's home was unremarkable—at least from the outside.

Had I known the park where I often jogged was the shady guy's clandestine drop-off point for top secret intelligence, I'd have been a lot more eager to hit the trail most mornings. And you can be sure more than physical fitness would have been on my agenda.

Turns out Robert P. Hanssen, F.B.I. agent and long-time Vienna resident, had been selling secrets to the USSR and Russia for over twenty years, in exchange for cash and diamonds. According to the Department of Justice, Hanssen, loyal husband, father of six and upstanding member of his church, was discovered to have been responsible for possibly the worst intelligence disaster in our country's history.

Enter intrigue, drama and eventually Hollywood. Our quaint little village was smeared all over both national and international news, and friends from around the world began contacting me with probing questions about my neighbor the double agent. We townspeople began wondering how well we really knew each other as we considered the espionage case that had been transpiring under our noses. "The Spy Next Door" took on new meaning.

Within a few years, after talk about the notorious espionage incident had died down, movie crews pulled into town. The film *Breach*, based on the Hanssen case, was being shot on location in the nearby drop-off park, and the town buzzed with renewed exposure to the limelight. A friend and I tried to get parts as extras—naturals jogging or shoveling snow near the park, but failed to make the cut. We settled for watching set designers spread fake snow around the park for Hanssen's winter, early morning drop-off scenes, hoping for sightings of famous actors like Laura Linney or maybe Ryan Phillipe, starring as a reporter and Hanssen's assistant, instrumental in helping to bring the traitor down.

Meanwhile, our infamous neighbor had been sentenced to life in prison on fifteen counts of espionage. Word around town was his wife had shared with fellow parishioners that her husband, in solitary confinement, was slowly losing his mind in a maximum security prison in Colorado. When asked if she still loved the man, she reportedly answered, "I pray for his soul every day."

If all this drama were not enough for our early days in Virginia, the entire world was traumatized on September eleventh of that same year. No place seemed safe anymore. As I tried to calm my children and convince them there really were plenty of good, kind, peace loving human beings, the elusive "Beltway Snipers" arrived on the scene. These were the two lunatics, a middle aged guy and his teenage partner, who for weeks drove around the district, Maryland and Virginia randomly shooting innocent bystanders. It bothered me that my children might be thinking all this violence and insanity was a normal part of life. Scared citizens no longer walked to their cars in parking lots, rather, instinctively zig-zagged like serpentines to avoid being the sniper's target. We were advised to duck behind our car doors when pumping gas, and most outdoor activities were cancelled following the release of a letter from one of the snipers stating, "Your children are not safe, anywhere, at any time."

And to think I had romanticized a cozy, comfortable, Mayberry-style life in our lovely new home.

After all, we'd been promised—"*Virginia is for Lovers.*"

Moping and Mopping

Ten years had passed and Virginia was beginning to feel like it might be my final resting place. This was the longest our family had ever stayed in one spot. With both kids off to college and my husband commuting to Texas for work, I'd grown weary of my humdrum life as a has-been homemaker. It was a dreary day in late October when I woke up, stared into the mirror and announced to my blurry reflection "You are getting a job this week!"

I considered the unfamiliar world of retail. It didn't take me long to come up with a potential employer. One of my favorite stores in the massive mall nearby was a rather unique shop hawking more gizmos and gadgets than one could imagine, along with furniture and home accessories. The place offered something for everyone and I convinced myself I could sell it while having some fun and making what I considered "lipstick money."

I dressed in what I hoped would come across as proper business attire for a salesperson, a celadon green cashmere sweater, black slacks, and sensible pumps. At the store I realized my sweater matched the walls of the store, which I took to be a positive sign as far as my new career in retail.

After requesting an application, I plopped down on one of the plush leather, oversized display sofas and began completing the form. I agonized over whether or not to leave the "criminal record" space blank, deciding my twenty minutes in the clinker for curfew violation back in Idaho was insignificant. I left the papers with an associate who promised to pass them along to the store's scheduling manager, a woman named April—a dim wit I will quickly come to think of as "April the fool."

I was barely in the door of my house when my cell phone began buzzing. I answered, identifying myself.

"Hello, Nan, this is April calling from RETRO-VERSIONS," a female voice bubbled. "I have reviewed your application form. How soon can you come in for an interview? We are currently hiring for the holidays and might like to have you on our team. We are looking for top-notch employees. Are you energetic, passionate, and hard working? Do you like to have fun?"

She seemed to be reading from a script.

I tried to sound effervescent, which is not my nature. I tend to be reserved, which did not seem to my advantage at the moment. So I forced with as much zest as I could muster, "Oh yes, definitely, yes!"

How else did she expect me to answer?

My interview was scheduled for the following morning and in the same outfit, I secured a position with what I believed was one of my favorite retailers.

Almost as quickly as I landed the job I changed my mind about the store. Within days of joining as a "Sales Associate" I came to think of the work place where I would toil away all week as a sweatshop. In retrospect, I realized I should have asked more relevant, direct questions during my initial ten-minute interview with April. Questions like, "What time do we get to leave at night?" Instead of the more specific, "what time does the store close?" And "How much will I be paid per hour, April?" rather than the vague "Does the store pay more than minimum wage?"

I say this because in reality there were too many grueling, long nights when after dusting and mopping and folding rumpled towels and sheets I'd drive home in the wee hours of the morning in worse condition than if I had been at a bar drinking for eight hours. Assured store policy required that I be escorted to my car should I work past nine p.m., more often than not I found myself alone, dashing through some dimly lit parking lot while keeping an eye out for strangers ready to jump me.

Turns out I actually made sixty cents per hour more than minimum wage plus receiving an employee discount of forty percent. This sounded like a great deal until I realized most every item in the store is so overpriced I could do better shopping elsewhere.

The low point of my high hopes for a career in retail came in early November after having been scheduled to work the 3:00 p.m. until closing shift. This meant I would work the sales floor until the doors were locked to customers at nine, at which point I would be forced to help close the store, which, depending upon the manager that night, might be well after midnight.

I quickly learned "closing" meant thoroughly cleaning the entire store, all six spacious sections. This included dusting the endless shelves, mopping the sticky hardwood floors, and rearranging merchandise, which sloppy, rude customers tended to carelessly toss about the place. We were also responsible for restocking all shelves, bins, baskets and counters with items stored in the hell hole of a stockroom in the rear of the store. This area, with its filthy, bug-infested kitchenette, cluttered, disorganized shelves, spilt paint, and broken glass, should have been condemned by both the health and fire departments.

One day in a rush through the stockroom, I slipped in a pool of spilt "Silver Sage" satin wall paint, ruining my comfortable new black suede clogs, purchased for this job requiring that I stand for what seemed like days at a time. I was not reimbursed for my loss, but scolded for leaving silverish footsteps throughout the hardware section.

My first night on the "C" or closing shift, I took the opportunity once the doors were locked to exert my creativity in the home décor department. I enthusiastically began rearranging the luxurious, colorful Turkish towels, plumping jewel-toned Thai silk pillows to toss across sofas and fake beds, and removing photo frames, ashtrays, candlesticks, and other knick knacks I considered to be clutter. I was enjoying myself as the clock ticked on and Ruth, the manager, counted and stacked piles of receipts and bills at the center cash register. So far she had not noticed what I was up to.

Suddenly a kind young Asian man named Shin who was moonlighting after his school teaching job, cautiously approached me whispering.

"What the heck are you doing, girlfriend?"

"I am making things look more pulled-together and attractive," I innocently replied.

"Don't you know we have a *BIBLE* we must follow here, Nan? Everything must be arranged EXACTLY according to this book," he stated emphatically while grabbing a large loose-leaf black notebook full of pictures and instructions.

I shrieked. "How boring! Talk about stifling my creativity!"

"Just get stuff back in order before Ruth notices, or you are dead," my confidant sternly suggested. "I will try to distract her for a few minutes."

I had been warned about Ruth, a tall, lean bullet of a woman. She had introduced herself to me on my first day, scowling, "I am Ruth, I am an Associate Manager and have worked in retail forever. I am a spinster."

I was not sure how to respond, but thought about replying, "Well, hi, nice to meet you, Ruth. I am a lowly, inexperienced Sales Associate, but I have a husband."

Instead I simply offered "Hi, nice to meet you. Would you mind showing me how to handle returns?"

Sometime after 11 p.m. I felt like the three of us peons had the store in good shape so headed toward the disgusting back room to grab my coat and purse and punch out on the clock. Noticing the direction I was headed, Ruth, who from that moment on I began referring to as "Ruth-less" barked at me across the floor.

"Where do you think you are going, Miss Kilmer?"

I so wanted to correct her. "It's Miss-us, Miss Ruthless."

"Well, Ruth, I am headed home since it is nearly midnight and I am parked at the far side of the mall. I do not want to be walking alone in the dark to my car in an empty parking lot much later than this. And, by the way, April assured me I would never have to walk to my car alone after dark. Is that right?"

"That is nonsense," Ruth hissed. "We are big girls and we can make it on our own. Just watch your back. And we are NOT finished here. Have you scrubbed the toilet yet?"

"WHAT?" I asked in disbelief. "Are you kidding?"

"I am certainly not," Ruth insisted. "This is in your job description."

I lost my cool at this point.

"Ruth, I have NOT been given a job description, and if I wanted to clean toilets I would have looked for a job as a chamber maid."

I did not bother to add that not only had I NOT been given a job description, I was also not informed that midnight janitorial work like dusting and mopping would be expected of me.

I seriously pondered why I ever wanted the job and the fact that I have a master's degree.

With that, both my co-workers and I grabbed our belongings and exited the store. Ruth-less, whose scarlet face looked like she might ignite into a bonfire at any moment, stared in disbelief.

I was somewhat hopeful as I made my way through the frigid,

deserted, scary parking garage that I might have just completed my last day in retail.

Alas, reminding myself I am not a quitter, I dragged myself back to the grind the next morning at ten sharp.

It went downhill from there. Ruth-less stalked me by day and harassed me at night. Fatigue sometimes exaggerated my annoyance with this unpredictable, often cruel creature, who I quickly concluded suffered from a common mental illness involving extremes of mood.

Ruth-less had a pet peeve, which was sales people in the stock room. The idea was that all staff out on the floor must wear radio headphones, to be able to talk back and forth with the stock room help and each other, ordering whatever a customer might need without physically walking back to fetch the item.

While this often-broken rule made some sense as far as avoiding traffic congestion and mass chaos in the stock room, it was painfully awkward for us salespeople. We'd have to idly stand by avoiding eye contact with an antsy customer, waiting for what seemed like forever for requested merchandise to arrive at the register. We were unable to help the next customer in line as the register would be tied up, so were forced to watch nervously for the lackadaisical stock boy to saunter out from the rear of the store, possibly with the requested item.

His job was not easy. For example, he might have to plow through mounds of discarded merchandise in the stockroom, hoist himself up the fifteen foot ladder to the shelf holding countless boxes of cabinet knobs in varying styles and sizes, hobble back down, maneuver back through the mess while slipping in spilt paint or a spilt soda, then cheerfully appear at the register desk with what were often the wrong knobs. It happened daily.

We carried a popular line of wall paint in vivid hues and varied finishes; I mentioned earlier I had ruined a pair of shoes in it. I was advised that whenever selling a gallon, I needed to double bag each can because one time, a woman purchased a large container of "Cappuccino" and the handle of the sack broke as she left the store. The lid popped off when the paint hit the floor, and the slobbering can rolled across the main hallway of the mall and into the foyer of Banana Republic. Gooey, dark brown paint oozed under shoppers' tired feet.

Needless to say, the mall management was not happy nor were those patrons who slipped and slid through the sticky mess while shopping for luxuries.

Just maybe there was an even lower point in my short-lived career at the mall. It was a biting cold December night during the Christmas season rush and I, as usual, was assigned the closing shift, so naturally I expected some sort of a fiasco. Ruthless was in a particularly irrational mood and after she slammed and locked the front doors, I watched her slowly, methodically sort the day's receipts. She bundled bills and cursed under her breath as she closed down each of the store's four registers. Meanwhile, I and the others, Shin, the Asian guy, and James, a dashing young investment banker by day turned salesman/janitor by night, set to work. We slaved along with Jonathan, a college drop-out and a nice enough kid I could not definitively label as retarded or genius. We commenced mopping floors, dusting lamps, tables and display cases, smoothing bedding and plumping pillows. Jonathan was especially skilled at folding the plush towels lining the walls of the store, and seemed content to be doing so. The rest of us restocked gadgets, gizmos and anything else running in low supply on the sales floor while Ruth watched from eyes we all were convinced were in the back of her hot head.

Despite the hectic day behind us, late hour, menial chores and Ruthless, we tried to remain upbeat as we hummed along to eighties tunes blasting from the store's sound system.

It all happened so suddenly I forgot to breathe. Without warning, Ruth SLAMMED a register drawer shut and stormed toward the stock room, her face growing a deeper shade of crimson with each pounding step. While the rest of us forged on with our chores in hopes of getting home before daybreak, the mad woman came reeling out of the backroom carrying a large, industrial sized, nearly six foot long mop. Carefully balancing the stick in the air as if spinning plates in the circus, she began to shriek.

"Obviously no one has demonstrated to you the proper way to mop, Miss Kilmer! So listen up! Shin, you need to watch as well!"

I can only pinch out the words, "Ruth, I have dusted the entire floor tonight. I used the smaller, absorbent Swiffer mop because it reaches under furniture and into corners, and is easier for me to handle."

Ruth-less did not seem to hear me. She firmly believed the larger mop was the better one, so I listened as calmly as I could to her lecture on proper mopping. Shin simply dropped his feather duster, grabbed his jacket, and announced, "That's it!

I have had it! I quit!" and walked out of the store. Part of me wanted to follow Shin but once I commit to a task it is nearly impossible for me to give up. We officially closed up shop a little after 1 a.m. and I could not wait to fall into bed after the most harrowing day ever. At home I collapsed into a deep sleep, comforted by the fact that the following day I was to work the early shift, and should be off by 8:00 p.m.

But not all the news for the next day was good. Ruth was working hours that overlapped with mine and the moment she caught sight of me, she began watching every move I made. When I got the chance, I sneaked into the stock room thinking the wicked woman was involved with a customer. I wanted to take inventory for myself so I knew where to locate whatever my customers might need. I rummaged through the disarray of stainless toothbrush holders and toilet paper hangers and soap dishes and shower curtain hooks, assessing the BATHROOM section of the mess. Suddenly I felt a presence next to me. There she was, pretending to be looking for a bath brush.

"Should you be back here, friend?" I hated when she called me this and wanted to slap her fiery face. I ignored her comment as I'd just found the polished nickel toilet paper holder my customer requested. I turned to bolt back to the front of the store as Ruth yelled after me "Kilmer! I NEED you on the floor! Customers are waiting!"

I thought to myself, "And they would be waiting a heck of a lot longer should we all choose to wait for a lazy stock boy to find the right merchandise."

Realizing that I was not wearing the mandatory radio headset, Ruth again approached me with a forced grin, clenched teeth.

"Where is your radio, Nan?"

"There are none available, Ruth. *So* many people are working today I could not find one, sorry."

"Well then *sweep* the floor and find one. Someone must've laid one down somewhere, so go find it!"

Sweep? Mop? What next, I asked myself.

I "swept" the floor as told and found nothing but a broken headset sitting on the filthy lunchroom counter. Ruth was not satisfied and remained hell-bent on finding me a radio. Less than an hour later, she appeared at my side with a headset sans earpiece.

"Here, put this on ASAP," she snapped.

I snatched the radio from her and attempted to attach it to my belt but realized the hook was missing. So I tucked the little box into the waistband of my slacks as Ruth stared in my direction with what I interpreted as a gloating look of accomplishment.

Minutes dragged past, customers came and went. Fragile glass holiday ornaments crashed to the hardwood floor, babies cried, sales people rang up sales, phone callers asked incredibly stupid questions and I needed to use the restroom.

Tense and in a hurry, I did not want to make antsy customers wait any longer than necessary. So I dashed into the ladies room, unzipped my slacks and promptly dropped the stupid radio into the toilet, which I noticed had not been flushed by the previous user. Panicked, I grabbed a pair of latex gloves from under the sink, pulled one on and retrieved the wet, slimy radio from the bowl.

"Now what?" I asked myself.

I quickly rinsed off the instrument under the sink faucet, dried it with several paper towels and stuck it back in the charger in the stockroom. Any questions and I would simply tell part of the truth—"That radio is not working."

Trusting no one, I kept this mishap my little secret. Later in the day I smiled as I caught good old Ruthless smacking the same radio against her knee, then holding it to her ear and trying to talk into the damaged transmitter.

I did notice the piece eventually dried out and worked again but was extra careful from then on NEVER to use the radio with the missing belt hook . . .

Every now and then someone famous at least by local standards appeared in the store to browse and shop. One day early in my employment a movie critic from the NBC local news station came in to shop for a wedding gift. He was very patient and kind and once I had rung up his purchase, he inquired as to whether I might be able to wrap the gift, a plush set of white Egyptian cotton bath towels.

"My wife would be forever grateful and so would I," he pleaded.

"No problem, sir. Just give me about ten minutes and I will take care of your package."

Heading back to the stockroom wrapping table I was more than grateful for a few minutes of respite from the general public. I carefully assembled a large, elegant gift box and as I attempted to assemble the lid slashed my right pointer finger, blood oozing from the cut. Horrified at the thought of staining the snowy white towels I grabbed a gold logo sticker from a roll hooked on the wall and smacked it on my finger in an attempt to halt the blood flow. A colleague came around the corner gasping at the sight of bright red blood. He guided me to the first aid kit in a cabinet nearby brimming with a disgusting assortment of junk and helped bandage my wound.

Quickly I placed the pristine pile of white towels in the gift box, wrapped a nice big grosgrain bow around it and took it out to present to the pseudo celebrity. He could not have been more appreciative. I cringed as I lowered the large box into a shopping bag and noticed my bloody fingerprints on the side. I pictured his grateful wife being delighted by the handsomely packaged wedding gift, then the horror on her face as she noticed the bloodstained box.

The kitchenette/lunchroom grew more disgusting each day. Not much larger than a typical public restroom stall, it was sandwiched between the two managers' offices off the stockroom. The place was an undeniable health hazard. Laden with stale moldy bread, half-empty soda cans, dead French fries and crumpled-up used napkins, the counters were filthy. Piles of dirty dishes crowded the scummy sink and the trashcan overflowed with plastic spoons, forks, cups and smelly fast food remnants. Though often not in plain sight, roaches, mice, and even rats must have been lurking nearby.

Since the Health Department did not seem to be interested in retail stores' lunch rooms, Ruthless took charge. One morning I arrived for my shift to find bright yellow "CAUTION" tape criss-crossing the door of the tiny kitchen, blocking my entrance to the room. I had wanted to squeeze my water bottle into the stuffed little fridge.

A large sign hanging from the tape read, "CONDEMNED! DO NOT ENTER!!"

Ruthless Ruth had had enough, and this time I did not blame her.

The room remained off limits for a few days before Amy the Manager ordered some poor lackeys to scrub it down and make it suitable for use.

Since eating in that infested hole was not an option for me, I had the choice: eating alone at one of the pricey restaurants in the mall; eating fast food at the food court at night, when questionable characters lurked and weary shoppers grabbed a quick, unhealthy meal; or bring food from home and sit in the center of the mall on a hard wooden bench feeling awkward.

Usually I tucked myself in a corner of a nearby Subway shop, put my aching feet up on the chair under the table and nibbled on one of those sandwiches that helped Jason what's-his-name lose over a hundred pounds. What a brilliant marketing strategy, I thought to myself, realizing I was beginning to think like a true retailer, for better or worse.

I ended up surviving roughly two months in the world of retail. I made my escape a few days before Christmas, much to the dismay of April the Fool, who harassed me until I walked out the door for the last time.

"This is NOT fair to the rest of us, Nan! We need you now more than ever!"

"Sorry," was all I could sputter.

It was years before I again entered my once favorite store, and never with the same eager anticipation. Instead I could only picture pitiful sales associates sweating while sweeping mounds of dust balls under the plump, fake beds, surly mangers demeaning diligent, well-intentioned subordinates, lovely cut-glass decanters crashing from overstocked shelves and hungry cockroaches snacking on crumbs in the filthy kitchen.

I stopped in one afternoon early in the new year to pick up my final paycheck and was greeted with chilly salutations, as if I were some shoplifter or bum.

Several new faces strained smiles from behind the counter, not realizing they might be filling my old shoes. I contemplated using my employee discount one last time, but decided I'd rather pay full price somewhere where I might get a little respect—without having to mop the floors, dust the shelves or scrub toilets.

Under Cover

My career in retail behind me, I am an aimless lady of leisure for several months when I meet a woman at a cocktail party who will become my next boss. As we chat she describes to me the job she has in mind. Her description sounds crazy yet tempting. It would read something like this:

WANTED: mature, professional, stable, licensed drivers 18 to 72 years old, to work for leading Defense corporation. Degree in drama, psychology, law, linguistics, physiology, logistics, cartography, mathematics, physics, education, philosophy, engineering, etc. desirable but not required. Computer skills a plus for interested applicants.

Ideal candidates should be capable of driving up to 90 m.p.h. while

—reading a tattered map

—operating a video camera

—changing clothes

—conversing via radio

Applicant also required to:

- — alter identity
- — change physical appearance including voice, gait, accent, mannerisms
- — run a five minute mile
- — convincingly lie/alter the truth
- — tolerate effects of alcohol
- — converse with strangers
- — complete detailed, legible, accurate reports
- — pass a polygraph test (for jobs requiring top security clearance)

I am drawn to Terri, a petite blonde woman who casually chats with me about job possibilities while we sip Chardonnay. She informs me she is a supervisor for surveillance specialists at a well-known defense company handling numerous government contracts. Intrigued by the intelligence world, I stagger backwards when she mentions the possibility of my working with her. And the suggested pay strikes me as ridiculously high, though I certainly wouldn't complain. What's more, Terri shares with me that in her experience she's found once people throw themselves into this type of work, the adrenaline kicks in and the rush is exhilarating.

My pulse quickens as she continues describing her work, not realizing she has already won me over.

The following day, as instructed, I send my resume to my new acquaintance. I attempt to enhance my professional bio by emphasizing my psychology degree, foreign language capabilities, physical fitness and social skills. I do not mention that driving fast is not one of my strong points. I figure I can force myself to accelerate when the time comes.

I wait nearly a year and decide this job is not going to pan out. In fact, I have almost forgotten about the possibility. Pondering other options, I answer my phone one winter day in late January, surprised to learn the caller is Terri from the cocktail party many months earlier.

"Nan, we met awhile back at the Graham's house, do you remember?"

"Yes, of course I do, Terri, good to hear from you. How are you?"

"Good, thanks. I have your resume here in front of me, and am wondering if you'd still be interested in coming to work for us?"

Before she could finish her sentence I blurt, "Sign me up! When can I start?"

Terri begins to explain, sounding urgent.

"The problem is I need someone immediately, Nan. Is it possible for you to fly down to Raleigh, North Carolina next Monday and spend about a week there?"

Glancing at my calendar I tell her, "No problem! But what exactly will I be doing down there?"

"Honestly, Nan, I have to tell you we are strapped for both time and people so I will have to ask that you meet a few of my colleagues at BWI airport on Monday, and they will brief you on the work to be carried out in the Research Triangle area. They will also have your hotel and transportation information at that time. Any other questions? I have another call waiting."

I am at a loss as to what I should ask on the spur of the moment and don't want to blow this incredible opportunity. So I simply agree to follow her directions and assure her, "Uh, I have no questions at the moment. Guess I will just wait for you to send me my flight information, and wing it from there!"

Eager to dive head first into an intriguing adventure, I hang up the phone and start making a list of things to pack for a week in North Carolina.

As I contemplate my new career in the undercover world, I am clueless as to what lies ahead for me over the next several years. And with the work I do not yet know how to do being classified I wonder how much I will ever be able to share for fear of jeopardizing national security. Later I will be relieved that I would not be required to take a lie detector test, as mine will be a lower level entry position. I think about all the paper clips, pencils, paper, erasers, staples, tape and even a pair or two of scissors I've "borrowed" from various employers over the years, and fear I might never be able to pass a polygraph given my shady history.

I make it through a crazy week in Raleigh not really knowing what I am doing. But within about six months I have spent sufficient time in "on-the-job training" to feel fairly comfortable in my new line of work. My duties are carried out either on foot or by car; each assignment varies. I much prefer walking over driving, as I can carry out surveillance activities while getting in miles of exercise, plenty of sightseeing, more than a lot of people watching and a nice tan, weather permitting. Driving around in a rental car is not nearly as appealing, especially in the heavy traffic of the larger cities we tend to navigate.

Although I am instructed not to share details about this clandestine job, anyone able to get to the Spy Museum in downtown Washington, D.C. can, for $9.95, pick up a copy of the *Handbook of Practical Spying* and learn all the simple techniques used in my line of work. It perplexes me why I must be secretive about activities that are or can be common knowledge.

Suffice it to say most of my days are spent following targeted individuals without them realizing they are under surveillance. I observe and assess their activities and demeanor, then compose reports for our clients, most of whom are government. We tend to work in pairs and are instructed to remain as unattached and inconspicuous as possible at all times. It does not take me long to master changing my clothes and entire appearance in a compact rental car with a man I might have just met, leaping out of a moving vehicle, and walking briskly for miles, often without eating or using a restroom for hours at a time. I find the job to be less than glamorous, but often lots of amusement and fun.

Normally I can find a topic of somewhat meaningful conversation with male co-workers who claim they are not watching me change clothes seated in a car next to them. One day I might switch from a navy blue linen dress, leather sandals and blonde wig to a black Adidas jogging suit, baseball cap and Nike athletic shoes, all within the confines of a tiny white Chevy. The job has its challenges and I do my best to overcome them.

Most days I get my wish and am assigned work on foot, often in desirable areas of the Washington D.C. area like Georgetown, Old Town Alexandria and downtown Bethesda, Maryland. I am not a large woman and tend to be rather quiet, so I guess no one pays much attention to me as I amble around town. I blend into the crowd so the boss tends to put me out on the street for hours at a time and I have few complaints as long as the weather is not too unbearable.

Sometimes I have to pinch myself on days that go well. I am amazed to be getting paid good money to spy and eavesdrop on complete strangers, which I have loved doing since I was a kid. Other days the time creeps by as I sit in a stuffy car on a quiet street for hours, waiting for a “package” as we call our subjects, who might never appear.

My colleagues are mostly stable people. The company hires primarily by word of mouth, and most employees are sane, sensible and reasonably bright. The occasional whacko slips into the mix, but this is an exception. Some hires have retired from their primary careers; others are youngsters who opt out of college or a boring nine to five office job; still others, like myself are bored housewives with empty nests who need something to keep them sober and out of the shopping malls.

Referring to the job description outlined earlier, it is understandable why a wide variety of people are drawn to this kind of work. Off the top of my head, I can tell you I have worked undercover with a former physicist, chemist, professor, musician, accountant, New York City drug enforcement agent, janitor, six-foot ten-inch college basketball star, and a bubbly blonde NFL cheerleader. I also worked with a nurse, professional upholsterer, wallpaper hanger, ballerina, rocket scientist, financial consultant and numerous retired lawmen, lawyers, pilots, and more than a few retired teachers, happy to be free from the classroom. With the C.I.A. nearby, it is natural for retired agency employees to enjoy this sort of gig; most are naturals and often share more than intelligence.

The Magic Wig

Towards the end of my first year on the job I am approached by my supervisor regarding several issues. First, I am instructed to buy a few more realistic wigs to alter my appearance. I have been using a conspicuously fake- looking auburn number that practically screams *disguise*. Second, I am offered a higher-level position that will require taking a polygraph test. And I assume I must pass it as well.

The thought unnerves me.

With this promotion comes added stress. I quickly realize a polygraph test incites intense, debilitating anxiety for skittish people like me, and realistic wigs and wardrobe disguises come at considerable cost. My employer does not offer reimbursement.

I am off duty one sweltering afternoon in July, so I decide wig shopping might be a fun outing for me and my teenaged daughter. Caitlin goes along as my consultant and after skimming the Yellow Pages we opt for a shop I've noticed in a strip mall near my yoga studio.

BIG WIGS lives up to its name when we get inside and realize it is considerably larger than it looks from the street. We enter and realize it is not the small, cramped little hole in the wall we have imagined, but a narrow establishment sprawling back nearly half a city block. We enter and are suddenly surrounded by hair; wigs, extensions, and toupees of every style, shade, texture, length and price you can imagine. The hairpieces, some of them made of fake materials, others real human hair, are hanging from the walls high above, stashed in cupboards, perched on styrofoam heads atop shelves, displayed in fancy glass cases and piled up on counters. There are wigs galore.

When Caitlin and I headed out this muggy afternoon, we had imagined we were off on a madcap, crazy adventure full of laughs. But once inside this shop it doesn't take long for us to realize the majority, if not all, of the clientele other than myself are women in varying degrees of serious illness. Some are bald, others wear colorful baseball caps, straw hats, turbans and scarves to hide the results of some dreadful disease. This puts a real damper on our afternoon outing. We try to ignore these poor souls, most of whom are trying to find a hairpiece identical to the head of hair they once had or were about to lose and are intent on finding just the right wig to feel as normal as possible in such a predicament.

Browsing around nonchalantly, I try to look beyond those less fortunate than myself. Caitlin sits flipping through realms of catalogues with titles like *A Wonderful World of Wigs*, *Hairpiece Happiness*, *Crowning Glory*, *Life Changing Locks*, and one of my favorites, *Hair Today/Gone Tomorrow*, presumably for women with hereditary loss.

There are a few female salespeople and I have my eye on a tall, plump blonde in her mid to late twenties. She has a certain flair about her, like she can take control, choose the perfect wig and make anyone confidently gorgeous in under thirty minutes and two hundred dollars.

I wait until Sheri, who tells us she is a former beautician, is free to wait on me.

"Hi there, can how can I assist you, Ma'am?" she drawls.

I reply, informing her of my quest. "I am looking for something that will make me look like an entirely different person and NOT like, 'Oh my! There is a woman in a wig!'"

"I see," Sheri replies, looking rather puzzled. "And may I ask why you want to look like someone other than yourself?"

I go on to explain that I will be using the hairpiece for undercover work I do and she quickly drops the subject. I get the distinct impression she's had customers like me before—lots of them.

"Have you thought about going blonde, honey?" she asks as she sizes up my figure, complexion and dress.

I recall having tried on my roommate's brassy blonde dynel wig back in college and remember rather vividly that it made my olive complexion look orangish—like one of those poor girls who used "Q.T." back in the seventies when self-tanners first came on the market. It was not flattering.

"I cannot see myself as a believable blonde, Sheri, but whatever you say!"

She whips out of nowhere a streaked-blonde, layered, shortish number with bangs and wispy little hairs that flip at the nape. It reminds me a lot of Martha Stewart's hairdo and it crosses my mind maybe she wears an expensive, no doubt 100 percent human hair, wig for all those air brushed covers of *Martha Stewart Living*. Who knows?

It is a really, really good, natural looking hairpiece Sheri shows me. Even the scalp is convincing; it has an almost sunburned look to it, like it has spent a little too long in the hot summer sun, maybe lingering over lunch *al fresco* or taking a long walk on an exotic beach. I try to leash my imagination and focus on what Sheri is telling me. She takes her time in fully explaining the ins and outs of this quality hairpiece, how finely it is made, how to pull it on from front to back, how to cram my shoulder-length brown hair underneath the blonde and how to care for the wig when not in use.

At last I am able to tug the stretchy cap of human-looking hair over my scalp, madly tucking my brunette mane under the golden helmet. Looking up at the mirror on the wall, I think I am hallucinating.

My reflection is a blue-eyed, perky *young* blonde with a revived, blushing complexion. The person in the glass looks vaguely familiar but I am not sure whose she is.

Caitlin glances up from her magazine. "Oh my gosh, Mom! I don't care how much that thing costs, you've got to buy it!"

"Let me style it a bit for you," Sheri offers.

She grabs a little wire brush from the drawer and begins fluffing, tugging and perfecting my new do. As she works, I casually ask her how she likes her job.

"I LOVE this work," she exclaims. "Sometimes it is sad to see so many sick people every day, but I find it most rewarding to help them look their best despite trying situations."

I think to myself, Sheri is not only a great salesperson, she is a good Samaritan as well.

I need no more convincing. I had set out on this shopping adventure vowing to spend no more than a hundred dollars on some sensible, believable wig. I end up forking over two hundred, in the interest of authenticity—not to mention looking younger. I do not, however, splurge on the rattan wig stand Sheri suggests nor one of those scary Styrofoam heads hairdressing students often use to carry around their "homework."

At home, I hang my stylish blonde prop at the foot of my bed. I wake up in the morning and seeing it makes me smile, realizing its exciting possibilities.

Commercials come to mind. *"Is it true blondes have more fun?"* Clairol asks its potential customers in its catchy sixties television ads.

"If I've only one life to live . . . let me live it as a blonde!" another successful commercial by the same hair care company declares in that same decade.

And then there are those other trite expressions about these "bombshells" like

"Gentleman Prefer Blondes." (But marry brunettes, I like to add.)

And notice how yet another ad campaign for Clairol, *"Does she . . . or doesn't she,"* features a glamorous blonde promoting the company's new "Hair Color Bath."

Confident and proud of my natural brunette-ness, these silly slogans fail to affect me as I go about my life. I give them little thought until now, as I don my new hairpiece and head to work this sizzling summer morning. I arrive at the "office", an undisclosed location in an underground parking garage somewhere in Northern Virginia. At first co-workers look past me, believing I am a stranger. On second look, eyes pop and brows rise. The first comment I get is from a female co-worker and it delights me.

"Oh my gosh, Peacock, you cut your hair! And I love the new color!"

Peacock, by the way, is my "handle" on the job. We all have these nicknames and truthfully I don't even know the real names of many of my colleagues.

Another older guy saunters over, staring at my head he whispers in my ear.

"Wow, I LIKE it, Peacock. You look real nice as a blonde."

I am mildly offended. Having spent my entire life with dark hair, I have come to believe I look perfectly fine as a brunette. After more crazy comments and commotion we all head out to hit the streets and my head begins to mildly throb as the wig seems to grow tighter and hotter with each passing hour. Not to mention the incessant itching.

I work until nearly midnight and arrive home to hear my husband upstairs in his study clicking away at his computer. He has been out of town and has not yet seen my new look, so I decide to surprise him.

Tiptoeing up the stairs to our bedroom, I quickly change into a turquoise "shorty" nightgown, still wearing my new wig. I slip into his office at the end of the hall while calling out in the most sultry voice I can muster, "What does a girl have to do to get a drink around here?"

He slowly swivels in his chair, forcing his eyes from his beloved computer screen. Catching sight of me sprawled on the sofa behind him, he jumps what seems like three feet into the air.

"OH MY GOD!" He cries, staring in disbelief as if he is trying to figure out what strange woman is lying in his study. "I THINK I LIKE IT!"

My feelings remain mixed. I am NOT a blonde and never wanted to be one. But duty calls.

Regardless, we get a good laugh and the relief is indescribable when I remove the golden shag from my itching, aching head. It has been a long day.

There are more blonde issues. My wardrobe has been chosen based upon being a brunette, and many if not most of my clothes do not compliment fair hair. My foundation looks a tad orange in the wig and my pink and coral lipsticks seem to fade to nothing without my dark hair as a frame. This bothers me. But nothing like what seems to be happening on the street. It is brought to my attention one afternoon as I am standing on a corner at a stoplight in downtown D.C., and from behind me I hear "Hola muchacha bonita, como estas?"

Puzzled, I look to my right and see a twenty-something-ish Hispanic "boy" making eyes at me. He and his little friend laugh as I dart off across the street visibly annoyed. At my age, this does not happen to me as a brunette—it hasn't in years. Judging from my new look, it seems men feel more compelled to heckle a blonde woman. I am thinking there must be some truth to the derogatory translation of "blonde" as loose, flaky, shallow, easy, whatever.

I once again remind myself, *"Gentlemen MARRY brunettes."*

Aside from these minor annoyances, I have fun with my wig disguise and am more often than not successful in fooling my targets while working undercover.

Some day I might invest in a copper-reddish and maybe a licorice black wig to further research the psychological effects of a woman's hair color on the male population.

Dōnde Estā Bloomingdale's?

Months pass and I become more confident in my work, wig and disguises, so I begin branching out, taking on some "special assignments" that require more knowledge and skill.

Early in the summer, a select group of us surveillance trainers are assigned a two-day gig that will kick off in midtown Manhattan. Most of the job will be conducted on foot as opposed to in vehicles, which I find appealing. Luckily, we arrive in the city and the weather is perfect for a day of adventure, which will take us from an undisclosed location in midtown Manhattan to the Bronx as our final destination. My colleagues on this job are some of the more entertaining, which usually makes for some fun times.

About a dozen of us gather outside the station at ten a.m. for our morning briefing. Afterwards, we all hop into two mini vans and head out to be dropped off at various spots around the city. As far as disguise, I am especially well prepared this morning with not three but four changes of clothing, several hats, matching shoes and bags, a nice assortment of accessories including rings, watches, earrings and belts. Of course I bring along my trusty blonde wig.

In route I decide to kick off the workday as a fitness buff jogging around the city. Using reverse psychology, I dare to wear an orange cotton sleeveless workout shirt, purple nylon running shorts, a lemon yellow baseball cap with SOUR PUSS on the brim, and silver and white NIKE "Zoom Airs."

I am assigned my "target" for the morning and sip from a water bottle as I saunter along behind him. No one seems to take a second look at me. I even pour a little water on the neck of my shirt so I appear to have worked up a sweat on my morning run. Details are crucial in my line of work.

Less than an hour into the chase I am fairly certain my package has noticed the colorfully dressed, middle aged, pony-tailed female jogger on his tail for too long. So I discreetly radio for a van to pick me up so I can quickly become a different person.

Once inside the van I struggle into a powder blue linen, short-sleeved dress appropriate for a muggy summer day in Manhattan, beige leather sandals, a matching handbag, dark glasses, a fake Rolex, my own gold and diamond wedding bands and let my own brown hair fall around my shoulders under a floppy straw hat. Even fellow co-workers who've known me for over a year walk right past without recognizing me, so I feel confident in this get-up.

Within minutes I am back out on the street, now meandering up Park Avenue and falling in behind my same target. He is not in the greatest physical shape and walks so slowly I feel I practically have to walk in place to keep pace with him. I am somewhat surprised when the "turtle," as I now refer to him, fails to hail a cab for some two hours this morning, and instead opts to leisurely walk the twenty or so blocks from Grand Central Station, where I initially picked him up, to the 59th Street subway station, where I discover he is boarding the Lexington Line, #5 train for the Bronx Zoo.

I join the slow poke window shopping along bustling, fashionable Madison Avenue. Every now and then I notice he seems suspicious of being trailed and see him peering into the glass windows, catching reflections. This is a hardly clever technique we professionals are taught to use as inconspicuously as possible while on the job.

I keep him in constant sight but at a far enough, strategic distance that he cannot spot a petite middle-aged brunette woman's reflection in the smudged glass.

I am gently swinging a silver Saks Fifth Avenue shopping bag where I keep essentials like my "walky-talky" radio, cell phone, sunscreen and ID. I have changed my gait to a sway, mimicking a confident, carefree woman casually shopping on a summer afternoon.

Once at Fifty-Ninth Street my target makes a "Romeo," or right turn, and we proceed east along the south side of the street towards Lexington Avenue, just a few blocks away. Once I realize the "turtle" is headed toward the stairs of the Lexington Avenue subway, I have to think fast. I must radio my boss right away and have her direct a nearby co-worker down the tube with our target. Chances are he has noticed me at least once back in midtown and will be suspicious if I show up with him on the #5 train to the Bronx hours later.

In an attempt to throw him off guard, I swish up beside him

and inquire in my best Spanish with an accent as thick as I can fake, *"Pardon Señor, pero dónde está Bloomingdale's?"*

This linguistic tactic has proven successful in the past, and I am proud of the skill. With Bloomingdale's little more than a block from the subway stop it would make perfect sense that a fashionable shopper might be heading to that renowned department store to pick up a new dress, a pair of trendy shoes or some high-end cosmetics.

Looking startled by my inquiry, the man, both hands raised to indicate helplessness, leans in closer to my face.

"So sorry, ma'am, I do not speak your language."

I reply in my best broken English, "Is OK, meester. I can understand the English!"

He at least understands Bloomingdale's, and kindly points me in the direction of the store. I hurry on my way. He seems convinced I am no one other than a harmless foreigner who doesn't know her way around the city but loves to shop.

Tea with Bin Laden

The dreaded polygraph test still looms in my not-so-distant future. In preparing for the grueling procedure I am up late one night scanning the Internet for information. I come upon "PASS YOUR POLYGRPAH TEST . . . I can show you how!" It reads:

"If you are getting ready to take a polygraph exam and are worried about it, then you have landed on the right page my friend. Over the past few years I have been showing individuals how to pass their polygraph examinations with ease. It is not hard to learn at all! Don't let this biased machine ruin your chances in life by falsely failing you. Protect yourself with the valuable information on this site."

I peruse the article and don't learn much that's new, nor do I feel more confident.

My cocky son has instructed me to simply clench my buttocks while answering each question to assure my vital signs remain constant regardless of whether or not I am lying. This bit of advice only confuses me, fueling my anxiety about taking the test.

I suffer from "White Coat Syndrome," so I fear this is a losing situation. When a doctor or any person in a white coat can raise my blood pressure by twenty, even thirty points, I can only imagine how I will react when wired, taped and hooked up to some lie detector apparatus.

It is a hectic day in August and I have spent the morning in the waiting room of an oral surgeon's office while my eighteen-year-old son has his wisdom teeth extracted. I am not yet aware that this will be the day I am subjected to a lie detector test, but I am already extremely tense just having to deal with a medical procedure. No mother enjoys having her child knocked out and cut up, myself included. I try not to think about the fact that some patients never wake up from anesthesia as I wait for my son to regain consciousness.

The procedure takes just under an hour, at which point a friendly nurse directs me to the small room where JP, minus four major teeth, lies on the table, his mouth stuffed with bloody cotton. Doped up and loopy, I realize that the kid would be a fun drunk. He is hilarious and has even the doctor in stitches—no pun intended.

Fortunately everything goes smoothly with the wisdom teeth extraction and I drive the patient home to recuperate for the rest of the day. It is around noon and I am barely in the back door holding up poor J.P. when I hear the phone ringing in the kitchen. I hurry to the phone, pick it up and some unknown person asks if I can be at a given location near Dulles airport within two hours for a polygraph test. I drop everything I have planned for the day, having been advised earlier that when invited for the exam I should make myself available at all costs.

Otherwise, my name will be put back at the end of the list and I might be forced to wait another six months to a year for the test. (Since September 11 polygraph offices across the country have been backed up for years while desperate employers are forced to wait for screened professionals.)

Reluctant to leave my poor kid alone, I nonetheless follow the precise directions given to me by the woman on the phone. I still get lost, so arrive in an even higher state of anxiety. While frantically driving, I worry that there is no way I can pass this upcoming test. Besides the petty theft I already mentioned, I tried pot a few times in college. But I swear even though I tended to hang out with the "druggie" crowd at Gonzaga, I only tried marijuana a few times and never really got into it. Something about inhaling a putrid smelling, foul tasting plant that burns your throat and lungs and stains your teeth just never really appealed to me.

I begin to think of certain so-called pathological liars I have known, individuals who do not even realize they are not being truthful and who in fact find reality quite boring. Like the new girl in sixth grade who told us all she was from Beverly Hills and that her family was moving to Nampa because her father owned a cattle ranch. Imagine our surprise when we later found out she hailed from Homedale, a tiny farming community some thirty miles outside of Nampa. At least this was a relatively harmless fib.

But there was also the disturbed guy from California who studied with me in Italy our Junior year abroad. He announced to a group of classmates one night in a trattoria in Florence, "Nan's parents met mine a few years back at Trisha Nixon's wedding. Right, amica?

In this type of situation I feel very uncomfortable and do not know how to react. I guess I should be straightforward and boldly tell the blowhard that he is lying. Or tactfully try to inform him that my parents do not know, or care to know the Nixons, and that surely he is mistaking them for another couple. Instead I changed the subject.

At any rate, I quickly review my past and conjure up mind-boggling stories I believe to be true and try to convince myself I am not one of these compulsive liars. Then I begin to wonder if a true compulsive liar actually believes she is telling the truth, would she not do well on a polygraph test? At this point I am nearing my destination and decide it best I drop all these rambling thoughts and focus on my mission at hand.

Once I arrive I am not only late but have no idea where I am. I have driven to a remote nondescript building a few miles west of the airport. Here I am frisked, directed onto an empty shuttle bus without windows, then whisked away to another unidentifiable gray concrete building five or ten minutes from the first. I am met by a tall, thin young woman in a professional gray suit and alarmingly petite black pumps so small they make me fear she might tip over.

My escort introduces herself by first name only, Faith, and invites me to use the restroom as she escorts me into the tiny, stuffy, stark cubicle where I will sit for the next four hours. (Hours later I will be glad I agreed to use the bathroom when offered.) Instinctively, I attempt to make light conversation with the woman but she only answers with one or two words signaling this is all *business*.

"Sit down and relax and I will hook you up to our equipment," the cold woman orders me.

As she closes the door and captures me in this cage of a space, I estimate my pulse to be around 110 and blood pressure well above what is considered normal and healthy. I try in vain to calm down and again try to reassure myself I have not told any significant lies or committed any relevant crimes in my past life.

I think I might be hyperventilating as the woman tapes magnetic clips onto my already sweaty fingers, strapping my torso to the stiff, cold chair and instructing me NOT to move or talk unless spoken to. The clips fail to adhere to my clammy fingers so she resorts to some sort of surgical tape in her attempt to measure my skin resistance, or Galvanic skin response, as she calls it.

I wait, half expecting her to call an ambulance once she gets a reading of my blood pressure. But her face shows no emotion, which I assume is part of her training. For nearly an hour she watches as a needle, which I cannot see behind me but can hear, clicks away in vain. I catch a glimpse of it during one of the several times she leaves the room for reasons she does not share with me.

"It is in your best interest to try to relax, so that we can complete this testing and get you out of here," my tormenter threatens.

It is around four p.m. when she leaves the room, as I squirm in my bondage, wondering how people with bladders much smaller and tempers less tamed can endure this grueling procedure.

Re-entering the closet-of-a-room, a perplexed, slightly frazzled looking woman, not looking me in the eye, stares at the long sheet of readings chugging out from the machine behind me. She cautiously inquires, "Would you be free to come back in tomorrow for further testing? I cannot seem to get a baseline reading for you. You should go home, get a good night's rest and return here tomorrow."

I want to tell her that all the sleep in the world will not help me conquer my fear of being wired up to any device. Put me in a doctor's office, strap that blood pressure apparatus around my arm, and panic shoots my numbers off the chart. As I stated earlier, I suffer from "White Coat Syndrome."

Frustrated, annoyed, and hungry, I half-heartedly agree to return the following day. The next morning I take the same cryptic route, pile into the same windowless van and am whisked away to the same nondescript building for more grueling hours of testing. Today I am met by a short young man with a military crew cut and beady little eyes darting through wire-rimmed glasses. He wears a tattered, ill-fitting gray suit and scuffed black business shoes, the toes curling up like an elf's. He behaves like a robot and offers no name.

"I see you have been here before, Miss Kilmer. So you know the routine. Would you care to use the restroom before we begin?"

I jump at the chance, this time knowing what lies ahead. I am taken to another room on a higher floor, identical to what had been my torture chamber the previous day.

The little robotic man has no more luck with me than Faith had the previous day.

The third person they brought in to wire me up seems to be trying to scare me and in this regard he is successful.

He is rotund, gruff and scraggly looking with unkempt salt and pepper facial hair. Judging from the small dents speckling his sallow complexion, he suffered from acne as a kid. He does not seem happy with his job or his life, for that matter.

The beast of a man begins his interrogation with nothing but, "I am Ralph and let's get on with this process so you can get out of here." At which point I thought I might ralph.

In order to get some sort of baseline reading I am required to as truthfully as possible answer such mundane questions as "Is your full name Nancy Lynn Kilmer?" to "Is George Bush President of the United States?" to "Is this the month of July?"

As is my nature, I assume I am being taunted with trick questions so try to out-think them thus raising my anxiety level even further.

Next come the real questions.

"Do you possess any knowledge that might be a threat to the United States?"

"No."

"Have you had any contact within the past year with any known terrorists?"

"No."

"Have you, in the past seven years, been convicted of a felony?"

"No."

And so on, and on, and on . . .

At one point, the by now visibly irritated man stops his probing questions and inquires, “Why is it, Miss, that you tense whenever I mention the word *terrorist*?”

I pause and cannot believe I have to respond to this absurd question. But I answer seriously.

“Rarely a day goes by that I do not worry about terrorism, and when you say the word I stress. Okay?”

Ralph does not respond to my honest statement. I feel as if he is looking right through me.

But my favorite question of the entire session is classic. The beastly man asks me with a straight face and a steady voice—“What would you do if Osama bin Laden invited you for tea?”

I can barely contain myself but manage to retort, “Oh my gosh, is he still alive?”

At this point matters intensify. This senior expert they’ve recruited in an attempt to obtain a valid reading on me loses his patience altogether. I stare blankly at the wall in front of me trying not to show my frustration and disdain.

“What are you hiding, Miss Kilmer?” he barks. And I can almost hear the polygraph needle screeching across the screen.

Now trembling with a stew of emotions, I again attempt to be straightforward.

“Nothing that I can think of, sir,” I offer with as much respect as I can fake.

He repeats, “Is there anything at all you are hiding from me now?”

Exhausted, uncomfortable and starving, all I can do is admit I am writing a book that some might consider a danger to national security.

Now I have piqued Ralph's interest and after another hour or so of intense conversation as to the contents of my story, he does not suggest, but orders me to turn my manuscript into the "authorities." My precise instructions are to deliver the stack of typed pages to a "drop off" sight near Langley so that the book can be read by an expert and screened for any breach of security.

At first I refuse this ludicrous demand. The thought of some poor slug sitting up late at night, nodding off as he is forced to read through my silly stories strikes me as beyond absurd.

Eventually I comply and deliver the stack of papers that is my manuscript, with the working title *The Magic Wig* to the designated site along with a brief cover letter.* To this day I swear this likely never-to-be-published work poses absolutely no threat to our nation's security.

In the end, the suspicious manuscript is supposedly "lost."

And within a few months I am informed that my polygraph test results are officially "inconclusive."

Thus ends my short-lived spy career, as I have no desire to retake what I have concluded is an absurd test and huge waste of my time and energy and our tax dollars.

*July 18, 2007

To whom it may concern,

Enclosed is a copy of **The Magic Wig**, a manuscript I drafted over one year ago.

I was administered a polygraph test on July 10 and 11, 2007. At that time I was instructed to submit my written work to this location.

I am told this material must be reviewed before I can be given a security clearance to carry out contract surveillance work.

I look forward to your response to this submission.

Sincerely,
Nan C. Kilmer

August 28, 2007

To whom it may concern,

Enclosed is a duplicate copy of **The Magic Wig**, a manuscript I drafted over a year ago.

I phoned you today, as it has been over a month since my first submission and I have received no response. I have been informed you misplaced the first copy of my work, which I personally delivered to this location on July 18, 2007, as instructed.

I have been informed this material must be reviewed before I can receive my security clearance to conduct surveillance work.

I was administered a polygraph test on July 10 and 11, 2007. At that time I was instructed to submit this manuscript.

Again, I look forward to your response.

Sincerely,
Nan C. Kilmer

Oddly, this package must have been "misplaced" as well. I received no response and abandoned any further efforts to obtain a security clearance.

What Hurts

My fear of being taped and wired up for a polygraph should not come as a surprise, as I have always been highly apprehensive about most any procedure some stranger might want to perform on me. I don't care for random people touching me, let alone being poked, probed, pinched, squeezed, wrapped, weighed, measured, or cut open. Add fear of doctors to my list of phobias.

Waiting for a doctor in a stuffy cubicle stresses me far more than, say, being in an airplane soaring thirty thousand feet over a bottomless ocean. My thinking is that within minutes a person in a white coat can doom me to a lifetime of pain, suffering and dreadful medications. On the other hand, if, in the unlikely event the airborne 747 jetliner I am trapped inside crashes into the deep dark sea, I have only a few terrifying moments of terror before it is all over.

I attribute my "White Coat Syndrome" in part to our family physician who delivered me and cared for me through my formative years. Dr. Ross, while a nice, rather funny guy, did not believe in painkillers. I swear if I'd had to have surgery as a kid he would have cut me open while I laid wide awake, in shock not only from the severity of the pain but the mere thought of what the doctor was doing to me.

Suffering from a grossly infected ingrown toenail as a child, it was painful to wear close-toed shoes, which was a problem during frigid Idaho winters. So my mother took me to Dr. Ross, who simply looked at my red, swollen big toe oozing a thick yellow fluid. Without warning the brusque man grabbed a little metal fork-like device, shoved it under the nail of my big toe, yanked it up out of its bed and stuffed a wad of cotton underneath, as my entire foot erupted in excruciating pain. The throbbing member spurt bright red blood mixed with the disgusting pus. I whimpered as the doctor instructed my mother, "Take her on home and keep clean cotton packed under that nasty nail for four or five days. Change the dressing three times a day whether she likes it or not. If the pain gets too bad give her an aspirin or two and for God's sake make sure the next shoes you buy the kid are big enough!"

I silently cursed the doctor for weeks as I suffered the worst pain I had known. I wondered if my long, difficult, breach delivery had forced him to perhaps miss his tee-off time, thus he held a grudge. Actually, I feel sorriest for my mother, having heard her description of my rough entry into the world.

There have been other incidents over the years to instill my distrust of physicians or most anyone in a white jacket affiliated with the medical profession. Although I guess I should be grateful to Doc Ross for preparing me for the natural childbirth I would experience years later in Asia. Having been refused any medication during the delivery of both of my babies, I had been forced to endure more pain than imaginable. People would commend my bravery after each birth, to which I'd respond, "I had no choice—but thanks a lot!" Admittedly, I felt fine immediately after giving birth, and could have gone out to work in the rice fields.

I have never had the wrong kidney removed, a surgical clamp sewn into my stomach, or even an incorrect medication prescribed for a misdiagnosed disease. But I fear all of the above plus more and carefully monitor any medical procedure I am forced to endure. But there is only so much I can control even though I own several medical reference books including my favorite, *The Merck Manual of Diagnosis and Therapy.* This voluminous publication is updated annually, with the claim: *"Provides useful clinical information to practicing physicians, medical students, interns, residents, pharmacists and other health care professionals in a concise, complete and accurate manner."* The manual is like a bible for hypochondriacs, Iatrophobics, (people like myself with an abnormal fear of doctors), and those generally concerned with the quality of health care in our country.

I recently subjected myself to my annual, dreaded mammogram. Given my high tolerance for pain I do not find this procedure especially uncomfortable. It is the humiliation of private body parts being wedged between two slabs of cold steel that bothers me. And questionable results can send me over the edge.

My latest procedure went more smoothly than it has in years. No waiting, a friendly, chatty technician and what seemed to be fewer films taken of my mammary glands.

I left the radiology building feeling the relief I always experience after a medical procedure, expecting as usual to receive a letter in the mail within four or five days reporting on the outcome of my mammogram. For some mysterious reason, this year I did not fret quite as much about the upcoming results as in the past. However my relative peace of mind was not to last long.

On the second day after my office visit I found in the mailbox the envelope with the return address, "Washington Radiology."

"This is unusually quick," I said to myself as I ripped open the letter. My eyes immediately scanned the few paragraphs and focused on the opening sentence of the letter.

"Your mammogram performed this past week is considered incomplete. In order to complete the evaluation, we need additional imaging studies."

At last I knew my fate. But I refused to panic and tried hard not to dread my upcoming diagnosis. If in fact it were cancer, I knew they had caught it early and I would most likely not die from it, at least not right away. Rather than worry, I chose to develop in my mind a plan of action.

I would not wear telltale wigs, not even the natural-looking blonde one I'd purchased for my undercover work. I would instead wear attractive hats and tasteful scarves which would be much more comfortable, knowing full well the torture of wearing a wig. I would endure chemotherapy like a trooper and support fellow cancer sufferers and survivors. I would become an activist for the cause. I would prevail.

I wait several anxious days for my follow-up imaging session, and after my repeat boob smashing I am escorted into a small waiting room where I find three other women nervously chattering, twitching and watching the clock. We have all been instructed to sit here until the radiologist has read our latest films and can give us results. Under tension these women seem to want to chitchat. One pudgy red head woman in a sailor dress with the top slipping down to expose a dingy white sports bra wants to share her daughter's life with me. Her twelve-and-a-half-year-old plays soccer and broke her right ankle in three places while skateboarding the previous week, at a family picnic at Great Falls Park, so will have to take the year off. And I should realize that soccer is her daughter's life. But she is not too worried about her recall today as she has extremely fibrous breasts and "nine times out of ten they take a second shot" as a precaution. She babbles on . . .

A second woman tells me she has already lost one breast so jokes that "another one gone would just be a balancing act." Her laugh strikes me as maniacal.

The third captive is the oddest of all. She is anorexic skinny with thinning hair dyed coal black which tinges her paper-white complexion a dingy grey. The slim foot crossing her bony opposite knee is pumping up and down faster than I can blink. Glancing up at me from her magazine she announces, "You know, if you were to hug me right now you might break one of my ribs!" She fakes her laugh and I, my smile.

She explains to me that she has broken most every bone in her body at some point, so is used to sitting in doctors' offices and is not at all anxious right now.

Her nonchalance is not convincing. I silently diagnose her with severe Osteoporosis, and would like to assure this pathetic creature that I am not even considering giving her a hug, but would like to treat her to a good meal.

Instead, I compliment her shoes, which are four-inch stiletto, black patent sandals which she is able to maneuver despite claiming having broken her left foot into two, separate pieces eighteen months earlier, hobbling her for most of a year. With this proclamation, a unanimous gasp permeates the room.

Thankfully, I am given the results of my repeat mammogram while I wait in the office, and am awarded a clean bill of health.

"There was just a tiny fold in that left breast so we could not get a good, clear reading the first time. You are perfectly fine—see you next year!"

I feel rather guilty as I pass the tiny waiting room after hearing my results. Compelled to poke my head in the door of the waiting room, I address the one lonely-looking, emaciated woman still waiting for her verdict.

"It was nice talking to you and I hope your news is as good as mine," I chirp, attempting to give her some hope. "Best of luck to you!"

The rail of a woman faintly smiles up at me, then looks back down at her glossy magazine full of beautiful, heathy, carefree people. Her frail image haunts me for days.

I know firsthand that medical care in other parts of the world is often inferior. While living in Bangkok I knew a woman who made the mistake of having her annual mammogram performed there. She was alarmed to say the least when one of her films showed a suspicious spot on her left breast. After some deliberation she flew home to Pennsylvania for a biopsy to be performed there by her personal physician. Imagine her reaction when a radiologist at her hospital informed her the spot on her film appeared to be grease, possibly from some type of fried food. We all concluded that her Thai technician must have been consuming a working lunch the day he was reading the x-ray in question.

I might be more than a tad phobic with regards to medical issues, but defend myself in that I still endure annual physicals by a gynecologist and internist. But I draw the line at dermatologists. With my decades of swimming, lifeguarding and sun worshipping, I realize this is not wise. Maybe in the fall when my deadly tan has faded I will see a specialist for a complete body screening. I'd like to avoid a condescending, lengthy lecture on the dangers of ultraviolet rays. I have heard it all before, and am afraid it's a little late in the game for me.

In the Mood

I had never known anyone who claimed suffering a stroke might be pleasant. That is, until I became familiar with the writings of Jill Bolte Taylor, a Harvard-educated brain scientist who claims some stroke victims can be left feeling perfectly content, depending upon the location of brain damage. She reports in her intriguing little book, *My Stroke of Insight*, that destruction of the left hemisphere of the brain can leave one feeling perfect, whole, beautiful—as if at one with the universe.

Taylor suffered a massive stroke at the age of 37. She writes that after a hemorrhage flooded the left hemisphere of her brain, she was tempted to wallow in the blissful solitude of her right brain. However, as an expert on cerebral functioning, the wise doctor knew enough to fight the peacefulness she initially experienced, so the left portion of her brain might heal itself. After a valiant uphill battle, she eventually recovered.

In laymen's terms, Taylor describes the predicament she experienced following her stroke. With only the right lobe of her brain functioning, the world shrank into oblivion. She was left in a state of being rather than doing, no longer thinking in language but in pictures. There was no need for analyzing, questioning, or even caring. The world as she knew it was perfectly fine.

How I wish I'd read her remarkable story earlier and known that my father might have been content to sit in his motorized chair or shuffle about with the aid of a three-pronged cane for thirteen years, unable to talk or move the right side of his body. As with Taylor, his stroke severely damaged much of his brain's left lobe, although he was no neuroscientist and probably did not realize it was in his best interest to fight complacency.

Incapacitated, he might have viewed his world like this:

Can't talk? What the heck; point and eventually you'll get what you want.

Can't walk? Plop down on the nifty motorized cart; it's fun.

Maybe, just maybe, Dad was at one with his universe and not as miserable as we might have imagined.

Even before his stroke, what my father did not say impressed me more than what he said back when he was able. Reid Kilmer was a man of few words. People said he resembled Steve McQueen in his better days, with his platinum hair, poignant blue eyes and crooked grin.

To me he was Dad and I adored him.

I must have been about five when one evening Daddy brought a couple of business associates to our house for dinner. After my mother's home-cooked meal, the men were sitting around our living room probably talking about work or sports or some other guy talk. Eaves-dropping from the top of the staircase, I was in my favorite blue and white cotton nightgown, floor length. I decided the nice men might enjoy some entertainment, so I slid down the banister instead of getting into bed as I had been told.

As the men took notice of me I proudly announced, "Watch me, sirs!" as I proceeded to stand on my head for our guests. I had forgotten underwear after my bubble bath . . .

All I could do was to run upstairs and try to cry myself to sleep.

Before long Daddy came to tuck me in with a goodnight kiss, as he did every night.

"Sleep tight, Nanner Poo. Don't let the bed bugs bite!"

That was it. No mention again of possibly the most humiliating incident of my childhood.

That was Dad.

My father and I had satisfying communication, often without words. On days when my mother was in a bad mood I could not wait until six o'clock. I'd listen for the station wagon to rumble into the garage and the back screen door to squeak open, and slam shut. Dad would saunter through the kitchen, gently tug my ponytail and grin as he pried open a Coors while leafing through the stack of mail. Mom would be peeling, chopping or frying as she chattered about her hectic day and unruly kids.

It wasn't easy to get my reticent father to tell me about things that mattered to me. Like flying bomber planes in the war, being Idaho's state champion diver, or playing football at

Nampa High School. Not a large man, he weighed in at around 150 muscle-bound pounds, yet held his own as a halfback for the fighting Bulldogs.

Dad's obituary appeared in the *Idaho Statesman* in 2002, and mentioned he was a World War II veteran, having served in the Army Air Corps and flown B25 fighter planes over Africa, Sicily, and Italy. People marveled. Most had no idea my dad was a hero.

Reid Francis Kilmer flew more than fifty missions in his bomber, the "Mississippi Gambler" before returning to the states. Alone, the spunky kid hitchhiked across North Africa to get himself on a ship full of fellow servicemen, at last headed home.

Sadly, while I was living in Bangkok in 1989, my father suffered a massive stroke while sleeping. Doctors gave him days, possibly weeks to live.

On the contrary, the tough old guy plugged along for more than a dozen years. He endured months of physical, speech, and occupational therapy, learning to live with only the left half of his body responding to his crippled brain's commands.

This meant learning to eat, dress, shave, comb his thinning hair, change the TV channels and write with his left hand. Communication was a challenge as his few words came out wrong most of the time. Family and friends fought the urge to second guess his comments and requests, as instructed by therapists. We were taught to be patient, to speak slowly and to offer multiple choice rather than "yes" or "no" questions. Something about the stroke victim's brain makes the decision between "yeah" or "nay" a tough one.

Our family tried to keep the mood upbeat around Dad, which was not easy. He could be confusing and unnerving. For example, a typical trait of a stroke survivor involves emotional response. Laughter and crying become simply a release of feeling—good or bad. He might cry at the sight of his favorite pumpkin pie, or laugh out loud when the neighbor's dog dies.

My parents made a good, solid team in their efforts to carry on as stroke survivor and caretaker, striving to make the best of an otherwise devastating situation. Dad made an effort to be a supportive husband even in his debilitated state. One particular Valentine's Day, my mother had briefly gone out to do errands, leaving Dad alone in front of the television with a snack and his beloved dog Tramp perched at the foot of his chair. Presumably, during this short time my father made his way to the kitchen, shuffling along with his three-pronged cane. There he found a brown paper bag in the drawer, and with his clumsy left hand, used scissors to cut out what roughly resembled a heart.

His next task was finding a pen, composing his jumbled thoughts, and scribbling for his bride,

"I lvo yuo."

When my father began suffering congestive heart failure, doctors gave him a month or two to live, so I booked a flight out to Idaho. There, I spent weeks sitting with Dad in the dimly lit den, serving his favorite foods and watching old *M*A*S*H* re-runs, Vanna White strutting about on *Wheel of Fortune*, and whatever mindless television his weakening heart desired.

One evening Mom was bustling around the kitchen before dinner as Dad and I watched Tom Brokaw deliver the nightly news. A small pot of tacky, plastic, battery-operated daisies sat atop the TV, a gift delivered to Dad during his latest hospital stay. By pushing a small button on the bottom of the pot, the famous Glenn Miller swing number "In the Mood" played while the flowers bopped up and down.

Dad, a smooth dancer, loved this Big Band tune.

Suddenly, the dying man seemed to bolt out of his chair, headed toward the plastic plant, three-pronged cane in hand. Before I could register what was happening, he poked the button on the flower pot, pulled my quivering body up from the loveseat, and we were jitterbugging.

This was our last dance.

The author, age 5, being ribbed by Daddy following dance recital.

The Front Line

No longer able to "cut a rug," Dad sat with me one afternoon shortly before he died. We were leafing through old family photograph albums when out of nowhere my mother hollered out from the kitchen, "Reid! As soon as you're gone I am getting a dog or cat!"

Dad and I exchanged grins.

As promised, Mom took in a straggly little pup not long after Dad had left this world. She rescued the pitiful mutt from an animal shelter, though many would argue the dog saved her from the lonely life of a widow. She and Pearl, as she called the motley blob of gray and white fur, were rarely apart during the final years of Mom's life. Pearl was a constant passenger as Mom tooled around town in her red Subaru, and sat dutifully beneath the table during weekly bridge games and dinner parties hosted by my mother for her slew of friends. Toward the end, the loyal pet refused to leave the failing old woman's side, even to devour dinner. It seemed our otherwise strict disciplinarian of a mother coddled her beloved pet more than she ever did her four children. Nothing had ever seemed to please her more than that silly little dog. They were meant to be together.

In the fall of 2013, our spunky mother left us orphans—me, my siblings and Pearl. Approaching her ninety-first birthday, the woman had lived a long and full life. The last visit I had with her, she confided in me with a raspy whisper, "Nanner, I am tired and ready to move on. I've lost my oomph. You know, I am never going to see you again, love. I want to—but I won't. It's time for me to give up and go."

Fighting for each breath, she ran her cold, bony little fingers up and down my arm a few last times as her sparkling jade eyes fizzled.

Stiffening, as if to hold myself together, I forced a smile.

"So you don't think I will make it up to heaven to join you some day, Mama?"

She grinned and coughed a crackly chuckle. A staunch Roman Catholic her entire life, the dying woman dumbfounded me with her blunt reply as she struggled to shrug her shoulders.

"Oh, heaven is a very nice idea and all, but who knows if it really exists?"

She gazed out her window as if waiting for my response.

Although crushed that Mom was not convinced she was on her way to eternal bliss, that "pie in the sky after you die" the nuns liked to promise, I had to believe even the most devout have their doubts. After all, Mother Teresa herself admitted to confidants that she was not always sure about religion and God. So I guess my pious mother could question the afterlife as well, though I refuse to picture her anywhere now but heaven, surrounded by other deceased loved ones and her favorite desserts, with soft jazz playing in the background.

Despite her powerful presence, my mother was a petite woman, weighing barely ninety pounds in the end. In her final months she'd lost her appetite for good, or I should say wholesome food. She'd barely touch most of the nutritious meals we tried to feed her as she grew more weary and frail. But desserts were her weakness and she'd never turn down favorites like lemon meringue pie, carrot cake smothered with cream cheese frosting and gooey ice cream sundaes.

In fact, Mom seemed to think the night before she died was cause for celebration. As one of her granddaughters watched from the next room, the little woman, oblivious to surveillance, proceeded to build herself a banana split. Sneaking around the kitchen like a mischievous child, she scooped herself a large dish of vanilla ice cream, smothered it and the counter in chocolate syrup, threw on some sliced banana, then swirled a hefty squirt of Reddi-Wip on top, sprinkling the sweet mound with a handful of peanuts. In her excitement, she forgot the cherry. Leaving the kitchen a sticky mess, she scurried back to her bedroom to devour the yummy concoction while catching one last *Jeopardy* episode. The sharp old gal still had most of the winning answers, right up until the end.

But the tenacious woman wasn't quite finished. Tiptoeing barefoot back into the kitchen, she dumped her walker and scrounged around in the pantry. Discovering a king-sized Butterfinger, she devoured the entire crunchy bar, purring between ravenous bites.

I figure it might well have been a diabetic coma that took my feisty mother in the end. But I have to believe she drifted off to eternity deliriously content . . .

A few months after Mom's "Last Sundae" my siblings and I were roaming around our parents' hollow house, sorting through what was left of their lives. Basically, besides some dog food and the remains of Mom's rubber band collection, only piles of photographs remained. We had divided up, donated, or destroyed most of their worldly possessions, and jointly decided to burn images of the past. We figured faded pictures of strangers wouldn't convey in the sale of the house, plus we'd kept duplicates of the more meaningful shots.

I stared out at the grey skies of Idaho's "Treasure Valley" while stacks of glossy pictures collapsed into smoldering ashes in the fireplace. We kept the one portrait we own of our grandfather, my mother's dad who abandoned her before she was mature enough to comprehend this was not what a father should do. She'd spent most of her life wondering about him, searching for him and hoping he'd return one day, if only to show his face, see hers, and disappear again.

Part of me would like to believe Mom might finally run into her dad in heaven, if it turns out there is such a place. But I doubt the louse would make it there given his performance here on earth. Still, we felt compelled to keep the photograph of this elusive man we never knew.

Mysteriously, my parents' wedding portrait seemed to resist the flames, defying "Until Death Do Us Part." Having been together for nearly sixty years, they proved invincible. I retrieved the indelible photo from the ashes and gently tossed it into the dwindling "Save" box.

Eventually the family scattered, and I sat alone on the floor, half expecting Mom to holler at me for a nice, hot cup of tea or another throw. She could be so cold at times.

Instead, I talked to myself as the walls began to spin, sucking the air from the room.

"Face it, Nanner, you are on the front line now," I managed to choke out loud.

And from out of nowhere that familiar voice in my head scolded me.

"Just relax and breathe deeply. Everything is all right. You know you are not dying—yet."

Loose Ends

Only after my mother was gone was I able to assemble the pieces. After a lengthy, tearful phone conversation with my godmother, Mom's dearest friend in Atlantic City, I came to understand the simmering tension between my mother and hers. And why, when as a snippy teen I'd mustered the courage to ask Mom if she actually liked her mother, she hesitated before answering. "Well. Let's just say I loved her. She was my mother. But I did not approve of her."

I surmised perhaps this was due to the fact our grandmother did not attend mass and was a fallen-away Catholic, thus mortal sin stained her soul, barring her from the gates of heaven.

Growing up, all I had been told was the story about my grandfather's mysterious disappearance. I knew my grandmother had been forced to work to support her child and herself, and that my mother was basically raised by her beloved Irish grandmother. Generally, Mom always described her life as brimming with fun, friends, and adventure, albeit missing a father and siblings. So when her four kids squabbled, as we often did, she'd scold us. "Do you have any idea how I longed for a brother or sister when I was young? You brats don't know how lucky you are!"

I did not give much thought to the situation other than the fact my mother had never been able to uncover anything about her biological father and dealt with abandonment issues all her life. As I matured, I was able to analyze some of the woman's behavior, like how she seemed to demand more of me and my sister than my two brothers. I figured she feared she'd better tread lightly or these beloved males might leave her as well . And when I turned twenty-one, Mom unnerved me with some peculiar advice. "Always choose a man you know loves you more than you love him."

Whether or not my godmother knew she was sharing a long-hidden secret, or whether Mom had asked her to reveal the shameful reality she endured as a child, I will never know. By the time I'd processed the information and wanted to inquire, my godmother had slipped into senility and no longer made much sense. The last few times we spoke, she badgered me. "Why doesn't your mother ever call me? I am very cross with her!"

In the end, I prefer to think my maternal grandmother made ends meet by keeping company with certain gentlemen around town, men of means. When you think about it, it was not that different from those intriguing Geisha women I'd admired back in Tokyo.

It's not like Grandma was a tramp.

She simply worked nights.

The author's mother Margaret Marilyn "Lynn" Thompson Kilmer.
Atlantic City, New Jersey, 1944.

Acknowledgments

I'd like to acknowledge all my loyal family, friends, editors, illustrator and publisher, for enduring this often bumpy road with me. Besides my stories, I can only offer warm thanks and heartfelt apologies. No one ever said it would be easy . . .

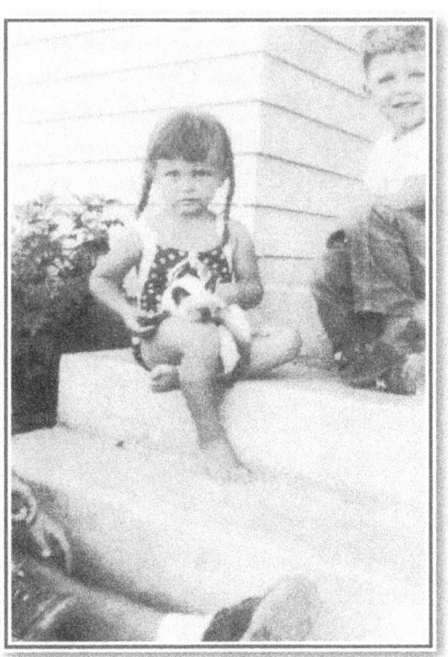

The author, age 4, cradling her kitten Jazzy.

www.ingramcontent.com/pod-product-compliance
Lightning Source LLC
Chambersburg PA
CBHW060631080726
47818CB00026B/348/J

* 9 7 8 0 9 9 7 7 7 9 5 0 9 *